A Justice Primer

A JUSTICE PRIMER

THIRD EDITION

DOUGLAS WILSON
& RANDY BOOTH

CANON  PRESS

MOSCOW, IDAHO

Published by Canon Press
P.O. Box 8729, Moscow, Idaho 83843
800.488.2034 | www.canonpress.com

This book is for

MARINELL and NANCY,

two pastors' wives *par excellence,*

who have had to deal with

more than their share of ecclesiastical gunk,

and who have done it with grace and style.

He is the Rock, His work is perfect;
For all His ways are justice,
A God of truth and without injustice;
Righteous and upright is He.

Deuteronomy 32:4

CONTENTS

to the
SECOND EDITION

I n the Spring of 2015, Canon Press published the first edition of *A Justice Primer*. In December of 2015 it was widely publicized that portions of the book contained some plagiarized material. I immediately took full responsibility for the problem and publicly acknowledged and apologized for my careless but culpable mistakes, having used some old material from a sermon that had not been properly cited in my notes at the time. As a result, I did not recognize that the material was not my own. *It was my obligation to be sure that this did not happen.* My co-author, Douglas Wilson, also apologized. And Canon Press publicly apologized, immediately pulled the book from publication, and conducted a thorough review. They "determined that the plagiarism in *A Justice Primer* was not the result of intentional malice." A few of the items that had been pointed out turned out to be minor citation errors that were easily corrected. The remaining material (less than four hundred words), has been deleted or rewritten for this second edition.

Sincerely,
RANDY BOOTH

EDITORIAL   NOTE

As this book was written by two authors, an appendix in this edition identifies the *primary* author of each major section.

EVERYDAY JUSTICE

God is just, and since we are made in His image, we too long for justice. Every child knows this early on, and thus it is common to hear the claim that something "isn't fair." C. S. Lewis observed, "Justice means much more than the sort of thing that goes on in law courts. It is the old name for everything we should now call 'fairness'; it includes honesty, give and take, truthfulness, keeping promises, and all that side of life."[1]

The demands of justice press us continually. We are called upon to render justice day in and day out: husbands and wives, parents and children, friends with friends, neighbors with neighbors, employers and employees, elders, judges, and juries. Everyone wants justice while few are well-equipped to render it. Nevertheless, doing justice is essential to all of our relationships within our families, churches, schools, businesses, and the civil realm. We want

1. C. S. Lewis, *Mere Christianity* (New York: Macmillan, 1952), 76.

justice for ourselves (tempered with mercy) but we are often careless with dispensing it to others. Our interest in justice is deep: because God is just, because we are created in His image, because we desire to be treated justly, and because we are obligated to treat others justly. This built-in sense of justice drives us back to its source. C.S. Lewis wrestled with the centrality of justice as he wrestled with God Himself:

> My argument against God was that the universe seemed so cruel and unjust. But how had I got this idea of just and unjust? A man does not call a line crooked unless he has some idea of a straight line. What was I comparing this universe with when I called it unjust? If the whole show was bad and senseless from A to Z, so to speak, why did I, who was supposed to be part of the show, find myself in such a violent reaction against it? A man feels wet when he falls into water because man is not a water animal: a fish would not feel wet. Of course, I could have given up my idea of justice by saying it was nothing but a private idea of my own. But if I did that, then my argument against God collapsed too—for the argument depended on saying that the world really was unjust, not simply that it did not happen to please my private fancies. Thus in the very act of trying to prove that God did not exist—in other words, that the whole of reality was senseless—I found I was forced to assume

one part of reality—namely my idea of justice—was full of sense.[2]

But what is *true justice*, and how do we get it? Is justice a simple thing, or is it hard to find? Are we as ready to render justice to others as we are to seek it for ourselves? The prophet says that God requires this of us: "He has shown you, O man, what is good; and what does the LORD require of you but to do justly, to love mercy, and to walk humbly with your God?" (Mic. 6:8).

What does it mean to do justly? The Bible has a great deal to say about this. Indeed, central to God's covenant with Abraham (and with us) is the condition of justice. "For I have known him [Abraham], in order that he may command his children and his household after him, that they keep the way of the LORD, to do righteousness and justice, that the LORD may bring to Abraham what He has spoken to him" (Gen. 18:19).

Proverbs 21:3 says: "To do righteousness and justice is more acceptable to the LORD than sacrifice." Moreover, Jesus warned: "Woe to you, scribes and Pharisees, hypocrites! For you pay tithe of mint and anise and cumin, and have neglected the weightier matters of the law: justice and mercy and faith. These you ought to have done, without leaving the others undone. Blind guides, who strain out a gnat and swallow a camel!" (Matt. 23:23–24). God insists on His justice being satisfied, even if it means the

2. C.S. Lewis, *The Joyful Christian* (New York: Macmillan 1977), 7.

death of His Son, and so too, must we take the issue of justice seriously.

NOT AS EASY AS IT MIGHT SEEM

At one level we can think of justice as "right and wrong," "true or false," "fair and unfair." Yet there are several factors and obstacles that go into achieving justice. Our ignorance, prejudices, emotions and agendas often pose the most serious threats. As with other knowledge, comprehending justice begins with the fear of the Lord. Proverbs 28:5 informs us that "Evil men do not understand justice, but those who seek the LORD understand all." Moreover, we are warned, "You shall do no injustice in judgment. You shall not be partial to the poor, nor honor the person of the mighty. In righteousness you shall judge your neighbor" (Lev. 19:15).

Justice often has to do with public accusations and charges that are denied by the one accused. When that happens, it is necessary for the accuser to be prepared to prove what he says. In order to do this, he must not be anonymous, he must be accountable for his charges (in case they prove deliberate falsehoods), and he must have independent confirmation of what he says. If these conditions are not met, we are prohibited by Scripture from even entertaining the charges (there must be two or three credible witnesses).

The perfect law of God has justice as its goal. When people are prepared to ignore, twist, or otherwise abuse the biblical laws of justice—often in the name of justice—the innocent are left unprotected. Biblical justice, i.e., justice rendered by way of the law of God, is a great expression of love. It is a primary means of loving our neighbors as ourselves as we show respect for God while seeking the good of our neighbors. False witness can be deliberate and malicious, but injustice can also be the product of carelessness and ignorance. If the result is injustice, then the innocent are destroyed regardless of the motive. We are called to self-consciously render justice, which does not allow for winging it.

The Westminster Larger Catechism, in addressing the duties and prohibitions attached to the ninth commandment, reminds us of the care that must be taken and the difficulty in achieving justice:

> **Question 144:** *What are the duties required in the ninth commandment?*

> The duties required in the ninth commandment are, the preserving and promoting of truth between man and man, and the good name of our neighbor, as well as our own; appearing and standing for the truth; and from the heart, sincerely, freely, clearly, and fully, speaking the truth, and only the truth, in matters of judgment and justice, and in all other things: Whatsoever; a charitable esteem of our neighbors; loving, desiring, and rejoicing in their good name; sorrowing for, and covering of their infirmities; free-

ly acknowledging of their gifts and graces, defending their innocency; a ready receiving of a good report, and unwillingness to admit of an evil report, concerning them; discouraging talebearers, flatterers, and slanderers; love and care of our own good name, and defending it when need requires; keeping of lawful promises; studying and practicing of: Whatsoever things are true, honest, lovely, and of good report.

Question 145: *What are the sins forbidden in the ninth commandment?*

The sins forbidden in the ninth commandment are, all prejudicing the truth, and the good name of our neighbors, as well as our own, especially in public judicature; giving false evidence, suborning false witnesses, wittingly appearing and pleading for an evil cause, outfacing and overbearing the truth; passing unjust sentence, calling evil good, and good evil; rewarding the wicked according to the work of the righteous, and the righteous according to the work of the wicked; forgery, concealing the truth, undue silence in a just cause, and holding our peace when iniquity calls for either a reproof from ourselves, or complaint to others; speaking the truth unseasonably, or maliciously to a wrong end, or perverting it to a wrong meaning, or in doubtful and equivocal expressions, to the prejudice of truth or justice; speaking untruth, lying, slandering, backbiting, detracting, tale bearing, whispering, scoffing, reviling, rash, harsh, and partial censuring; misconstructing intentions, words, and actions; flattering, vainglorious boasting, thinking or speaking too highly or too meanly of ourselves or others; denying the gifts and graces of God; aggravating smaller faults; hiding, excusing, or extenuating of sins, when called to a free confession; unnecessary discovering of infirmities; raising false rumors, receiving and countenancing evil reports, and stopping our ears against just defense; evil suspicion; envying or grieving at the deserved credit of any, endeavoring or desiring to impair it, rejoicing in their disgrace and infamy; scornful contempt, fond admiration; breach of lawful promises; neglecting such things as are of good report, and practicing, or not avoiding ourselves, or not hindering what we can in others, such things as procure an ill name.[3]

INJUSTICE

When the principles of justice are neglected, the result is most often injustice. Sometimes the injustice is the result of ignorance (which is less culpable because it is not high-handed). This sort of injustice stems from the fact

3. *The Westminster Larger Catechism*, Center for Reformed Theology and Apologetics, http://www.reformed.org/documents/w1c_w_proofs [accessed September 10, 2014].

that many Christian people have never been taught from Scripture how to separate and distinguish true from false, slander from honest report, or due process from a hatchet job. An accusation is not evidence. What we have heard is not the same thing as what we know.

However, some people cling to their way of "adjudicating" even though the scriptural principles are laid out clearly and repeatedly in front of them. Those who self-consciously embrace injustice this way do so because they are unjust men. Truth and argument to them are mere instruments; they will speak the truth if it advances their cause, and they will speak a lie just as readily. They will use the truth, they will ignore the truth, and they will display a reckless disregard for the truth. "Evil men do not understand justice, but those who seek the LORD understand all" (Prov. 28:5). Justice often involves hard work. This is another way of saying that injustice doesn't just fall from the sky. Injustice is an action or a set of actions performed by personal agents, and the character of the action derives its quality from the one who does it, and not the other way around. An adulterer commits adultery; a thief steals; a covetous man covets. In the same way, an unjust man does and speaks unjustly. "An unjust man is an abomination to the righteous, and he who is upright in the way is an abomination to the wicked" (Prov. 29:27).

Jesus taught us that sinful actions proceed from the heart of man. The fruit does not determine the nature of the tree; the tree determines the nature of the fruit. While

injustice is often the product of sinful ignorance and neglect, it also frequently proceeds from unjust men. Unjust
men are so for different reasons: some of them are driven
by their doctrines, some by envy or bitterness, others by a
desire for revenge, and so on. But all of these share injustice
in the heart, and injustice in the heart leads to injustice in
the hands and on the tongue. Beware of unjust men.

THE JUST AND THE UNJUST

The Bible tells us that the Father "makes His sun rise on
the evil and on the good, and sends rain on the just and
on the unjust" (Matt. 5:45). This is but a temporary mercy.
"Or do you despise the riches of His goodness, forbearance, and longsuffering, not knowing that the goodness
of God leads you to repentance?" (Rom. 2:4). "The LORD
is longsuffering and abundant in mercy, forgiving iniquity and transgression; but He by no means clears the
guilty . . . . " (Num. 14:18). In other words, God is a just
God, and His justice will be satisfied one way or another.

Once an unjust man settles upon some injustice, the
reports begin to circulate, and, not surprisingly, those who
love justice answer the charge. The apostle Paul had to
deal (repeatedly) with those who twisted his teaching out
of all recognition—"as we are slanderously reported and
as some affirm that we say" (Rom. 3:8). The devil is the
father of lies, and, not to put too fine a point on it, this
means he lies. Sometimes the lie is entirely false, but more
often the lie is mixed in with just enough truth to make

it hold together. And when the person charged attempts to explain (which he may need to do because of the "just enough truth"), the hooting starts; the buzzards begin to circle. Just men are judicious men; they are careful with what they say and careful with what they hear. The stakes are too high to do otherwise. However, those engaged in slander can almost never bring themselves to act in a careful and judicious way. Their hearts are tumultuous, and they generate tumult wherever they go.

Once the dispute starts, the disputants do not all share the same advantages. Those who love a lie are not constrained by facts and can fight dirty, or not, as it pleases them. They can twist a how-do-you-do into something sinister. They craft their accusations in such a way that any and every response is more proof of their claim. Truth, on the other hand, is constrained by its own nature and the bounds of Scripture. Truth fights by the rules, and lies fight lawlessly. This might seem like an insuperable disadvantage, but there is something else to consider: Truth fights under the covenant blessing of the triune God, while lies are in the service of the devil, who loves to double-cross and abandon his own instruments. When Judas was hunting for the rope, the devil wasn't trying to save him.

Nevertheless, in the short run, lies are much more flexible, and in the tussle the unjust are not above a little eye-gouging and ear-biting. The great Puritan writer Jeremiah Burroughs put it this way: "Truth is the bond that

keeps unity, but error is wild."[4] Because error is wild, the
best thing for truth to do is stay on the path, not turning
aside to the right or the left. Truth should do what truth
does the best, which is to move on straight ahead. Truth
fights when it has to, but it fights in the path, in order to
stay on the path. Bunyan's pilgrim was not chasing over
the meadows in order to go Apollyon-hunting. He fought,
but he fought because Apollyon was in the path. We have
our tasks assigned to us, and it is most important that we
remain faithful in those tasks, whatever liars may say.

---

4. Jeremiah Burroughs, *Irenicum: Healing the Divisions among God's
People* (Orlando: Soli Deo Gloria, 2003), 16.

CHAPTER 1

CONFLICT *and* JUSTICE

*Who is wise and understanding among you? Let him show
by good conduct that his works are done in the meekness
of wisdom. But if you have bitter envy and self-seeking
in your hearts, do not boast and lie against the truth. This
wisdom does not descend from above, but is earthly, sensual,
demonic. For where envy and self-seeking exist, confusion
and every evil thing are there. But the wisdom that is
from above is first pure, then peaceable, gentle, willing to
yield, full of mercy and good fruits, without partiality and
without hypocrisy. Now the fruit of righteousness is sown in
peace by those who make peace.*

JAMES 3:13–18

The history of man is one of conflict—whether past conflict or conflict lying in wait.[1] This conflict is but the fruit of the deep root of envy. "He has it and I want it, and even if I don't really want it, I don't want him to have it." The perfect (i.e., mature) man,

---

1. We are speaking here of moral conflict that arises from sin. There is a different kind of "conflict" or dispute that is centered on the "facts" of a matter (e.g., "It was raining this time last week." "No, it wasn't.").

Jesus Christ, was selfless. The immature and fallen man is autonomous and selfish. Adam and Eve envied God, and herein the first conflict erupted. They wanted to be as God; to at least be His peer. This conflict between Creator and creature led to a separation of mankind from God, from life to death.

When confronted with his sin, Adam compounded the conflict by pointing his accusing finger at Eve and ultimately blaming God for having given him such a wife. Together (in time), they would fill the earth with like-minded immature accusers.[2] A long string of conflicts ensued and has since comprised the story of man. "Then the LORD saw that the wickedness of man was great in the earth, and that every intent of the thoughts of his heart was only evil continually" (Gen. 6:5).

We live in a time when envy has been turned into a virtue. Jesus told the parable about the workers hired at different times of the day to make a spiritual point directed at envy (Matt. 20:1–16). But we take the side of the workers who labored through the day and would tend to see this as the basis of a class-action lawsuit. Nevertheless, Scripture declares, "A sound heart is the life of the flesh: but envy the rottenness of the bones" (Prov. 14:30). What motivated Joseph's brothers to seek his elimination? Stephen answers the question clearly for us. "And

2. Immaturity and selfishness are synonymous. Two two-year-olds in a room with one toy is the picture of immaturity or selfishness. Jesus is the picture of maturity, laying down His life for His friends.

the patriarchs, moved with envy, sold Joseph into Egypt: but God was with him" (Acts 7:9).

Envy was the driving force behind the persecution of the apostles. "But when the Jews saw the multitudes, they were filled with envy; and contradicting and blaspheming, they opposed the things spoken by Paul" (Acts 13:45). "But the Jews who were not persuaded, becoming envious, took some of the evil men from the marketplace, and gathering a mob, set all the city in an uproar and attacked the house of Jason, and sought to bring them out to the people" (Acts 17:5). Indeed, this root of envy led to the grand conflict of the cross. "For he [Pilate] knew that they had handed Him over because of envy" (Matt. 27:18). And the apostle Paul endured much conflict due to this kind of envy: "Some indeed preach Christ even from envy and strife, and some also from goodwill: The former preach Christ from selfish ambition, not sincerely, supposing to add affliction to my chains" (Phil. 1:15–16). "For you yourselves know, brethren, that our coming to you was not in vain. But even after we had suffered before and were spitefully treated at Philippi, as you know, we were bold in our God to speak to you the gospel of God in much conflict. For our exhortation did not come from error or uncleanness, nor was it in deceit. But as we have been approved by God to be entrusted with the gospel, even so we speak, not as pleasing men, but God who tests our hearts" (1 Thess. 2:1–4).

Even within the church, this root bears its ugly fruit: "If anyone teaches otherwise and does not consent to

wholesome words, even the words of our Lord Jesus
Christ, and to the doctrine which accords with godliness,
he is proud, knowing nothing, but is obsessed with disputes and arguments over words, from which come envy,
strife, reviling, evil suspicions, useless wranglings of men
of corrupt minds and destitute of the truth, who suppose
that godliness is a means of gain. From such withdraw
yourself" (1 Tim. 6:3–5). While we cannot always immediately identify the specific object that is being envied,
when conflict arises it is a safe bet to take the Bible's word
for it: envy is lurking somewhere. In the end, the envy
comes up empty-handed. "For the living know that they
will die; but the dead know nothing, and they have no
more reward, for the memory of them is forgotten. Also
their love, their hatred, and their envy have now perished;
nevermore will they have a share in anything done under
the sun" (Eccles. 9:5–6).

The man who envies desires what is not rightfully
his—all sin is a form of theft. When a conflict arises, it is
the job of justice to determine the rightful owner of the
thing in dispute. "Wisdom from above," which is rooted
in the truth of God's word, a wisdom that is administered
by those who are themselves "peaceable, gentle, willing to
yield, full of mercy and good fruits, without partiality and
without hypocrisy" (Jas. 3:17), is the way of justice. Justice
is found when those "who are of full age [mature], that is,
those who by reason of use [of the word of righteousness]
have their senses exercised to discern both good and evil"

(Heb. 5:14) are employed to make judgments in a conflict. This is the combination of a righteous, objective law in the hands of a righteous man. Good and evil are not so easily discerned apart from skilled application of the word of God. "Now the fruit of righteousness is sown in peace by those who make peace" (James 3:18).

THE MYSTERY OF SCANDAL

The word *scandal* is unfortunately common in Christian circles, but much of the modern use of *scandal* is not in line with the scriptural concept. We usually mean something important. But we haven't understood the biblical doctrine of scandal just because we have dealt with our own scandals (and it is a central doctrine of the Bible).

There are two kinds of scandals. The common kind occurs when a congregation, group, community, or whatever is tootling along, minding its own business, and some kind of drastic and scandalous sin erupts. Everybody has to deal with the aftermath of it, and there is a big mess. In the church, this happens when the youth pastor runs off with the choir director's wife. In a nation, it happens when the number two guy at Homeland Security is discovered to have been on the payroll of Al-Qaeda. In this kind of situation, some manner of high-profile wrongdoing suddenly intrudes itself into the life of that society. People are scandalized, deal with the problem (rightly or wrongly), and move on.

But in the biblical worldview, scandal is caused by the intrusion of righteousness, not unrighteousness. This "intrusion of righteousness" occurs in such a way as to reveal the violent and self-righteous basis for that culture's existence. This is why the cross is a scandal.

The former situation is in effect when a peaceful church is upended by some dramatic sin, and everyone is upset, but almost no one is confused. Everybody knows that it was wrong for so-and-so to have done thus-and-such. But the latter kind of scandal is almost certainly in effect when controversy, conflict, or disputes appear to be escalating without any sense of rationality at all. Almost everyone wants to know what is going on. "Surely this can't be it?" Nevertheless, the cycle of conflict continues to ratchet upwards. What is causing this?[3]

In the first scenario, the procedure that is outlined in Matthew 18 makes contextual sense. A man leaves his wife and kids; he is confronted by a friend, then by two or three witnesses, and so on. You are dealing with a discrete sin that has handles on it.

But how are we to understand the hopelessly tangled controversy involving scores or hundreds of people? What are we to do when the engines of the conflict seem to be invisible? Where is the energy for this disruption coming

3. In what follows, we are greatly indebted to the insights of Rene Girard, who ties together a number of smaller biblical themes, putting them together in an integrated way. A good introduction to some of Girard's insights can be found in his book *I See Satan Fall Like Lightning* (Maryknoll, NY: Orbis, 2001). But of course, in recommending his work, we are not going along with everything he says. Every author should be read with discernment. But for all that, Girard remains richly rewarding.

from? Many churches have gone through a dark time—a church split, a meltdown on the part of some of the members, or some variant of all that—where every overture of peace makes things worse, where every blessing to some is taken by others as a violent insult, where plain reason makes no difference, where people switch sides in apparently irrational ways, where the closer the parties are to each other the more violent the conflict, and so on.

What Rene Girard does so effectively is make the invisible engine visible. What drives this sort of thing? Read on.

A good way to describe this is to juxtapose the tenth commandment and a comment from James the Apostle. The tenth commandment says that we are not to covet anything that belongs to our neighbor, and James asks and answers a basic question for us. "Where do wars and fights come from among you? Do they not come from your *desires* for pleasure that war in your members?" (James 4:1, emphasis ours). Where does conflict come from? It comes from imitative desire.

The second greatest commandment, to love my neighbor as myself, is a summary of the second table of the law, commandments five through ten. Commandments five through ten culminate in the tenth commandment, which prohibits the only thing which would make disobedience of five through nine even possible: "desire for what belongs to my neighbor"—desired because my neighbor has it. Who has not watched two toddlers playing in a room whose floor is covered with toys, and one toddler goes over and picks up a toy in the corner that has been untouched all morning? Suddenly the second toddler has to have it, and the reason he has to have it is because his neighbor now has it. Before his neighbor had it, he didn't want it. This is imitative desire.

Another way of putting it is that all my ethical duties are to be fulfilled with regard to God in the first place and my neighbor in the second. The position of my neighbor in biblical ethics is profoundly important. And the closer I am to him, the more likely it is that I will be tempted to covet, want, and desire his stuff. Sometimes the desires are material; men want their neighbor's car, or house, or wife, all of which are certainly prohibited in the commandment. But the commandment goes on to cover everything—"or anything that is your neighbor's" (Deut. 5:21). This is where the source of the conflict can become difficult to see, because often my neighbor is in possession of certain blessings from God that are intangible. But the fact that they are intangible does not keep an envious neighbor from wanting them violently, even if he cannot see them. Some of the intangibles that are desperately wanted, or in the language of Deuteronomy, coveted, are things like a good relationship with a father, happiness, status, the position of being the firstborn, easygoing respectability, good looks, good fortune, etc.

So where does crazy, inexplicable conflict come from? "You lust, and have not" (James 4:2). We have counseled people before who were gracious, kind people, well thought of, obviously under the blessing of God, and their problem was an irrationally snarky sister, let us say. And the better they were to her, the worse it got. Where does this come from? It comes from lust, imitative desire. Not lust in the sexual sense, but a deeper, more profound lust, of which sexual lust is just a subset. This is the lust—the fundamental carnal desire—to be friends with the world (James 4:4). James goes on. "Or do you think that the Scripture says in vain, 'The Spirit who dwells in us yearns jealously'? But He gives more grace. Therefore He says: 'God resists the proud, but gives grace to the humble.' Therefore submit to God . . ." (Jas. 4:5–7a). This is the kicker, because after James analyzes the problem for us, what he tells us to do with it will only (at least in the short run) make things worse.

If someone is the recipient of a host of gracious intangibles, what is the result if his neighbor "wants" those? The result is inescapable conflict. And in many cases, it is conflict that cannot be erased because the gracious intangibles cannot be abandoned. If God is blessing someone, then God is blessing him, envious neighbors or not. What could Joseph have done to keep his brothers from being in conflict with him? Keep quiet about his dream, you say? The problem was not *between* Joseph and his brothers, it was much deeper than this. And it was so much the brothers' *own* problem, it would have come out somehow—regardless of what Joseph had done or not done. The blessing of God cannot be hidden away for the sake of the carping and envious onlookers.

Note what James tells us. There is conflict in the world that comes from lust, desire, and envy. He says that the spirit in man tends this way. This is not an occasional problem for the occasional person. It is pervasive, and we all have to deal with it. But God intervenes in our lives, and He gives "more grace." There are two kinds of people in the world. Both kinds are sinners, but one of them has received the kindness, forgiveness, acceptance, and blessing of God. The other category remains in sin—and God resists the proud, meaning that He does not give grace to them. He gives grace to the humble, those who submit themselves to God. Now if the initial problem was caused by a proud man envying the grace that had been given to another, what will happen if the gracious man understands this grace of God, and submits to it further, humbling himself? God will give more grace. And the proud man is now in the position of being resisted by God. This, in terms of the conflict, will only make things worse.

The more obviously God pours out His blessing, the worse it will get, at least for a time. In the case of Joseph's brothers, they finally came to repentance when the grace of God in Joseph's life was overwhelming. But this was also the grace of God in their lives. Prior to that intervention of God for their blessing, any blessings for Joseph did nothing but exacerbate the situation.

The ultimate example of this, of course, is the treatment that Jesus received. Never has a human being been so blessed by the Spirit of the Lord as He was. Never was there a man who spoke as He did. Never had the blessing of God been so evident in anyone, anywhere. And what happened to Him? His continuing to live in human society was obviously intolerable.

This reveals that "worldliness" is a profound commitment to resist and suppress the truth that righteous scandal reveals the emptiness and deceitfulness of the world. This is why the cross is the ultimate scandal, according to St. Paul. All secular cultures and civilizations are built on violence and murder, deceitfully covered up. From Oedipus to Romulus to the tombs of the prophets built by Christ's pharisaical opponents, civilized respectability hates any intrusions by the grace of God.

And when the grace of God is poured out in any place, one of the first things that happens is that reactionaries start to marshal their forces to attack and suppress things that nobody in their right mind could be against. All kinds of trumped up charges are alleged and circulated widely. The early Christians were accused of incest and cannibalism. And we have seen the same kind of thing. One of the funniest charges leveled against us in Moscow was the charge that everybody in our church was forced to make his own toothbrush. In Nacogdoches the rumor circulated that every new member was given a rod and instructions on how to use it. Where is all this coming from? The charges are one thing; the reason for them is another. And the reason for them is the appearance of blessing in human communities.

One other thing needs to be said: The grace of God is *grace*. In other words, there is no foundation in it for boasting anywhere. The ones attacking often do so because: "You think you are better than everybody else. You have that holier-than-thou smirk." To protest that "no, it is all a gift from God" only inflames the resentment further. "So why did God give *you* all that, and give *me* this?" Christians often think that if their blessings were the result of their own work, that would be the cause of the world's enmity. No, then the enmity would cease. The cause of the bitterness is resentment of the sovereign, efficacious, infinitely kind grace of God. Persuade an unregenerate enemy that you really don't deserve any of what you currently enjoy, and he will only hate you more. Persuade him that you did it all yourself and he will probably let you be—because maybe he could accomplish it, too.

In short, when St. James tells us where conflict comes from, he is not talking about the relatively rare kind of conflict where two men fight over a parking spot, two women over a man, or two dogs over a bone. These are examples of what he was addressing, but they are only the most obvious examples. James is teaching us about all conflicts and, in particular, he is explaining the mysterious conflicts, the ones we don't understand.

CHAPTER 2

STANDARDS *of* JUSTICE

Righteousness and justice are the foundation of Your throne;
Mercy and truth go before Your face.

PSALM 89:14

In the Supreme Court Building in Lausanne Switzerland hangs a painting by Robert Paul titled *Justice Lifts the Nations*. Justice points her sword at a book that is labeled, "the Word of God."[1] God's law is perfect, and it provides the perfect standards for justice. God is just. Justice is one of His attributes, a part of His holy character. As Greg Bahnsen put it, "the law is a transcript of God's character, one's response to the law is one's response to God himself."[2] It therefore establishes the standards of justice for those made in His image. One of the ways we express love for God and for our neighbors is

1. Francis A Schaeffer, *How Should We Then Live*, (Fleming H. Revell Co., Old Tappan, NJ, 1976), 106.
2. Greg L. Bahnsen, "The Theonomic Reformed Approach to Law and Gospel," *Five Views on Law and Gospel*, Stanley N. Gundry, ed., (Zondervan, Grand Rapids, MI, 1996), 94.

by upholding those standards; by doing justice and righteousness. "By this we know that we love the children of God, when we love God and keep His commandments. For this is the love of God, that we keep His commandments. And His commandments are not burdensome" (1 John 5:2–3). Doing right, protecting the innocent, and promoting the good are some of the goals of justice.

The infallible standards of justice include all of God's Word. None of His requirements is unjust, either too lenient or too harsh. The Bible provides a universal standard for all men, in all times and in all places. There is no double standard. As Bahnsen has observed, the Pharisees attempted to escape this by overlooking the weightier matters of the law, such as justice, mercy and faith (Matt. 23:23–24). But Jesus tells us that in so doing, they were "blind leaders of the blind" who transgressed God's law by supplanting it with their own traditions (Matt. 15:3–6, 14).[3]

A SENSE OF JUSTICE

Having been made in the image of God, every child is born with a powerful sense of justice or fairness. God's law is written in our hearts. However, we are also fallen and sinful creatures and thus our sense of justice has been perverted. It is slanted toward ourselves. Therefore, we are incapable (in ourselves) of establishing and maintaining

3. Greg L. Bahnsen, *By This Standard: The Authority of God's Law for Today*, (Institute for Christian Economics, Tyler, TX, 1985), 30–31.

true justice. We love ourselves, but not God and our neighbor. "Because the carnal mind is enmity against God; for it is not subject to the law of God, nor indeed can be" (Rom. 8:7).

Autonomy seeks to replace the perfect law of God—which is perfect justice—with our own standards of justice. Justice demands an authority. By what standard will we evaluate fairness? Who will execute or enforce justice? Is this standard and authority infallible? How are the standards to be applied? Who says? These are all inescapable questions. Some standards will be applied, and some authority will stand behind those standards. The alternatives are limited. Essentially, we can choose between autonomy and theonomy—man's law or God's law.[4] One of those standards will be the ultimate authority and arbiter of justice.

There are a variety of human courts: moms and dads, elders and ecclesiastical courts, and judges, juries, and the civil courts, to name a few. These are God-ordained authorities charged with justly applying God's standards. "Let every soul be subject to the governing authorities. For there is no authority except from God, and the authorities that exist are appointed by God. Therefore whoever resists the authority resists the ordinance of God, and those who resist will bring judgment on themselves"

4. Cornelius Van Til, *In Defense of the Faith, Vol. III, Christian Theistic Ethics*, (Presbyterian and Reformed Publishing Company, Phillipsburg, NJ, 1980), p. 134.

(Rom. 13:1–2). While these authorities apply the standard imperfectly, nevertheless, they do give us a certain type of justice. When one of these authorities finds someone guilty or not guilty, it brings order to the society they are ruling over. Given their human limitations, this kind of justice is also a limited justice.

THE GOLDEN RULE AS A GENERAL RULE

> Judge not, that you be not judged. For with what judgment you judge, you will be judged; and with the measure you use, it will be measured back to you. And why do you look at the speck in your brother's eye, but do not consider the plank in your own eye? Or how can you say to your brother, "Let me remove the speck from your eye"; and look, a plank is in your own eye? Hypocrite! First remove the plank from your own eye, and then you will see clearly to remove the speck from your brother's eye. Do not give what is holy to the dogs; nor cast your pearls before swine, lest they trample them under their feet, and turn and tear you in pieces . . . Therefore, whatever you want men to do to you, do also to them, for this is the Law and the Prophets. (Matt. 7:1–6, 12)

The fact that philosophers lack a foundation has not prevented them from trying to come up with improvements on the Golden Rule. And without granting that they are in fact improvements to the rule, we might still benefit from looking at the ancient problem of selfishness from new angles. Kant's form of it was the categorical imperative—behave in such a way that you would be willing for your conduct to become a universal rule. The legal philosopher Rawls put it this way: design the ideal society in your mind without knowing where in that society you will be born. This is the same approach taken by a wise mother who tells her son to cut up the pie for all the kids—and adds that he will take the last piece after everyone else has chosen.

When it comes to matters of justice in church trials, witnesses, and presbyterial hissy fits, we can adapt Rawls's exhortation. Design in your mind the ideal system for adjudicating troubles in the church. Do this without Rawls's democratic egalitarianism making a hash of it, and just sit down with an open Bible. Find out what the Bible teaches on this subject without knowing whether you will be the judge or defendant, witness or accuser.

What this removes is the very carnal (and very easy) tendency toward partisanship. What do we mean by partisanship? Say that your congregation is troubled by some of the standard afflictions of Zion, and you have two roaring factions. One of them wants the carpet in the foyer to be red, and the other wants it to be blue. Feelings are running pretty high, and many on both sides are starting to question the spiritual maturity of the boneheads on the other side of this issue. Now in the middle of all this, suppose that one of the most vocal members of the

blue faction is arrested by the cops for his extensive collec-
tion of child porn stashed in his basement. He was, before
this, a respected member of the church and nobody knew
about his sin.

There are two ways this could go. The easy way is the
partisan way. In other words, the members of the red faction, after the initial shock, start giving way to feelings of
quiet but increasing confidence. "This deals a deadly blow
to the forces of blue." While no one goes so far as to make
a direct link (as in, "support for blue carpet leads to child
porn"), the disaster is still used politically. Alternatively,
a tragedy like this ought to suddenly put everything into
perspective. "Whatever our differences in the past, we all
agree that this is horrible, that it must dealt with, and so
on." This "second way" is far more edifying and honoring
to God, but not nearly as useful politically.

So that illustrates what we mean by partisanship. Partisanship looks at whatever mechanisms for justice exist
and asks how these mechanisms can be manipulated to
achieve the ends that are desired. In this view, courts are
simply a tool of partisan politics. If it suits us, we demand
that it be used this way, and the next time we might insist
on the exact opposite. In other words, suppose that the
next week the chairman of the red carpet party got caught
embezzling from the offering. All of a sudden, the vocal
advocates of swift-and-certain justice with regard to child
porn are arguing that, when it comes to embezzlement, as
we learned in *The Merchant of Venice*, "The quality of mercy

is not strained; it droppeth as a gentle rain from heaven."
All this shows is that people who behave this way are not
interested in justice at all (or love, or mercy, or integrity),
but rather in getting what they want.

Now back to our ideal justice system. In a situation
like this, we are setting up the mechanism of settling disputes in the church without knowing at all whether the
Lord will cast us as the red faction, the blue faction, or the
elders of the church across the street who will inherit the
disgruntled blue party after the first church blows up.

What should the rights of the accused be? Answer
the question without knowing whether you will be the
accused or the accuser. What should the responsibilities of
the elders be? Tell me without knowing if you will be one
of them or not. What should the liability be for one who
bears false witness and slanders another? Give the answer
without knowing if you are the slanderer or the slandered.
And so on. We all know the principles of justice and have
them down cold when our interests are on the line. But
we tend to forget or minimize them when someone else is
being railroaded, especially if we have a partisan interest
in that railroading being successful.

We live in a fallen world, and the fall has affected the
administration of justice. The Church herself is by no
means immune from those distortions of justice. More
than one presbytery has frog-marched a man of eminent
holiness to the door. "And stay out!" More than one liar has
borne false witness in a church trial and gotten away with

it. More than one anonymous slanderer has harangued
the public with arguments so convoluted that they could
be used for deck screws. More than one rogue pastor has
established a mini-papal state and run it like Leo X on a
toot. More than one pietistic soul has torn apart a church
with all her damn prayer requests. All this is granted, and
then some. All this is laid on the table, and raise you ten.
Injustice can and does flow in any direction. This is not
to say that injustice flows everywhere all at once, with all
parties equally guilty all the time. Rather, we are arguing
that, at any given time, we do not know a priori who is in
the right and who is not.

Paul says that Timothy was prohibited from receiving
a charge against an elder without two or three witnesses
(1 Tim. 5:19). This was not because they were in authority, but rather because they were accused. In the biblical
world, the accused always gets the benefit of the doubt, always gets the presumption of innocence. This was not because of any assumption on Paul's part that elders couldn't
sin. No, because he goes on to say that if the conditions
were met, and the elder was convicted (on the word of two
or three witnesses), he was to be rebuked in the presence
of all so that the others would stand in fear. Peter tells
us what some of those sins of elders might be. "Feed the
flock of God which is among you, taking the oversight
thereof, not by constraint, but willingly; not for filthy lu-
cre, but of a ready mind; neither as being lords over God's
heritage, but being ensamples to the flock" (1 Pet. 5: 2–3).

Two sins mentioned here are greed for money and lust for power. Peter also refers to false teachers who are looking for a little action (2 Pet. 2:14). So there you have it, the three g's of ministerial abuse—glory, greed, and girls.

Because this is the way it is in our messy world, it is quite possible that men in authority have abused their position for power, for money, or for the sake of their lusts. But for exactly the same reason, it is just as easy to falsely accuse someone of falling when they have not. To accuse a minister of greed may well be false, but it is not absurd. And so we have to establish protections—protections for everyone. And we should go so far as to let just about anybody do the exegesis, just so long as they are ignorant of what role they will have in the upcoming trial held in front of them the entire time.

These matters are not hypothetical. Some of us have been maligned and misrepresented more times than Carter's got little liver pills. We also have friends around the country who have been in judicial meltdowns of various kinds, and we have had friends occupying different places in those meltdowns. We know conscientious pastors who have been slandered by parishioners. We know conscientious parishioners who have been slandered by elders. And we have heard of a fracas (from time to time) that doesn't concern us, and we do not want to take a passing dog by the ears.

So, to conclude, here's a little hypothetical scenario. You designed the system, God has placed you into a highly charged situation, and we are now test-driving your sense of justice: In our scenario, it turns out that you are falsely accused of child molestation. What is the Golden Rule and how did you apply it to the process? Did you write laws that allow for anonymous accusations to be made against you? Is there no accountability for the accuser if the charges are shown to be false and full accountability for you if they are shown to be true? Did the one bringing charges read only a selection of the primary documents? Before the indictment, were both sides heard completely? Did anyone settle on your guilt before they even heard your account? If so, Scripture says it is a shame and folly for them. But if such people are allowed to hear your case, in the courtroom you designed, it is a shame and folly *at the design level.*

CHAPTER 3

JURISDICTION
and AUTHORITY

Let every soul be subject to the governing authorities. For
there is no authority except from God, and the authorities
that exist are appointed by God. Therefore whoever resists
the authority resists the ordinance of God, and those who
resist will bring judgment on themselves.

ROMANS 13:1–2

"Jurisdiction refers to the bounds and limits of a source of legal authority."[1] This might include geography, government, and political or relational authority. The various spheres of authority have specific jurisdiction, or limits over who they are responsible for. For example, parents have authority and jurisdiction over the children of their own household, but not over the children in the household next door; elders have authority and jurisdiction over their local church but not over the church down the

---

1. "Overview of the Types of Jurisdictions," Laws.com, accessed August 1, 2018, http://court.laws.com/jurisdiction.

street; and the state of Texas has authority and jurisdiction over her residents but not over the residents of Idaho. Moreover, authorities are also limited in the kinds of
matters they may adjudicate. In other words, some things
are simply none of our business, and we need to stay out
of them altogether.

Authorities and jurisdictions do sometimes overlap,
and thus there are often multiple parties who have a legitimate interest in a matter of justice. In such a case there is
usually a hierarchy of authority that determines who has
the primary jurisdiction. It is the duty of an authority that
has jurisdiction to administer justice to all who are under
his authority. This is why an unjust judge is a terror to
those under his authority and jurisdiction.

Our notion of what is just often looks different from a
distance. The thirty-thousand-foot aerial view lacks preci-
sion. And while it might be correct in its perception, that
distant point of view is not the same as those with front-
row seats. Those with authority and jurisdiction are in a
position to see, hear, learn, compel, limit, and evaluate the
evidence and then to implement the safeguards necessary
to achieve justice. Authority can say yes or no, permitted
or not permitted, sustained or overruled. Authority is essential to the process of justice but is always limited in its
jurisdiction. It is easy for those in the cheap seats to question the call at second base, especially when the call goes
against their team. But, in the end, being "subject to the
governing authorities" means honoring their decisions.

Now there are exceptions to these rules since some authorities are corrupt or overreach their legitimate jurisdictions. There is a time, a place, and a way to object to such things, but even here the biblical standards of justice must prevail. The fact that we might think a particular ruling was unjust does not give us the authority or the jurisdiction to simply take justice into our own hands. Appeals might be made to other authorities who are in a position to evaluate the case and to provide some checks and balances. In such matters caution and care must prevail.

What about the jurisdiction issues raised by the multitude of churches, presbyteries, and so on? The principal answer to this is easy—but the devil, as they say, is in the details.

Christ requires us to be striving for likemindedness. This does not mean clonelike conformity (we worship a triune God, after all), but neither does it mean the all over the map pandemonium that is frequently characteristic of all the churches in the yellow pages (the Lord our God is one God).

We should begin with the most important acts of other churches that we ought to honor and accept, and that would be their sacramental acts. Christian churches ought to honor one another's baptisms, for example. Contrary to the assumptions of many, acts of church discipline are not at the center of our identity as Christians, while baptism is.

We should also reject the notion that acts of government should be honored or not honored based on that other church's similarity to us in their polity. If a man left his wife, and was disciplined by his Baptist or Anglican church, and fled to a Presbyterian church for refuge, the second church should honor the discipline even though it wasn't presbyterian discipline. We honor Christian baptisms that are not Presbyterian, so why not honor the lesser thing?

The only real question about discipline is whether it was just or unjust. If a church with a confession and polity identical to your own disciplines a man unjustly, then (after appropriate investigation) that disciplinary decision may be set aside. And if a man was disciplined for adultery (of which he was truly guilty) after a prophetic word exposed him down at Knee Deep in Glory Worship Center, that discipline should be honored. Of course, the ideal ought to be to have godly biblical procedures serving the intended outcome of those procedures, which is justice. So if the prophetic word was the only basis for the conviction, and the man involved denies his guilt, then that judgment should be overturned as well.

You can't make a good omelet with rotten eggs. It does not matter how good the recipe is, how good the cook is, how expensive the pots and pans are, or how high-tech the stove is. If the men involved are unjust men, they will simply use a first-rate kitchen as their instrument to stink up the place. All this to say that we must confess that rotten eggs can and do make it into the glorious kitchen of presbyterianism, and all the books of church order in the world can't alter the outcome.

One other thing should be noted about refugees flee-
ing from one church to another. Often the refugee knows
enough to cast his appeal in terms that are flattering to
the church he is appealing to. Suppose a man gets disciplined for his use of child porn, and the elders who disciplined him hate Calvinistic doctrine, which in no way
prevents them from having a biblical take on child porn.
So they excommunicate him. He flees to us and tells us a
story about how the real trouble was his sympathy with
Calvinism. Among other things, this kind of approach is
flattering (which is why a lying flatterer would use it). At
the same time, there have been godly Christians hounded
out of churches by ungodly sessions on the basis of that
session's wild speculations and doctrinal incompetence.

So the rule of thumb ought to be this: If someone
comes to you from another Christian church, and they are
under some kind of cloud, admonition, rebuke, suspension
from the Table, or excommunication, what this should
mean is that the burden of proof has shifted. An individual in your own church is innocent until it is proven that
he is guilty. Guilt has to be established, and it has to be
established beyond any reasonable doubt. But if another
church has taken disciplinary action of some sort against
one of its members, and then that member comes to you,
the burden should be on him to demonstrate and prove
that an injustice was done to him. If he can do so, and all
the principles of justice are remembered (with the former
body given full opportunity to present its reasons), then

there is no problem (in principle) with a receiving body overturning a judicial decision by another church.

In short, if Christ has not withdrawn His fellowship from someone, then neither should we. If Christ has bound in Heaven what was bound on earth, then we should not try to untie it. Honest sessions and presbyteries discipline liars who run off to other churches and tell lies. So be careful. Dishonest presbyteries heave godly saints out the door. Do not honor judicial outrages. The list of saints who have been treated unjustly by ecclesiastical assemblies is a long and honorable one.

CHAPTER 4

ACCUSED *and* ACCUSER

Do not keep silent,
O God of my praise!
For the mouth of the wicked and the mouth of the deceitful
Have opened against me;
They have spoken against me with a lying tongue.
They have also surrounded me with words of hatred,
And fought against me without a cause.
In return for my love they are my accusers,
But I give myself to prayer.
Thus they have rewarded me evil for good,
And hatred for my love.

PSALM 109:1–5

We commonly talk about the rights of the accused in matters of justice. But in the tangled web of human experience, the accuser can rapidly become the accused. Then what do we do? Often, if we like what an accuser under authority is doing, we call him a whistleblower. If we don't like it, we call him a treacherous sneak. But we should not call him anything until we know.

The first thing to do, especially for all internet observers, is to maintain a heart check that will keep partisan interests out of any situation. When someone accuses someone else, and someone else makes a counteraccusation back, the thing we must not do is take up sides based on other partisan considerations. Suppose a paedobaptist accuses a credobaptist minister of embezzlement. I am not to lean in the direction of the accuser because of our shared exegesis on the covenant. Take this a step further. Suppose an accusation is made against someone who is my personal adversary, someone I believe has wronged me in the past. I get word, say, that a parishioner has accused this particular pastor, who has previously come after me, of something nefarious. If my response were, "How sad. It was just a matter of time," I would be wronging that pastor in a grievous way. Keeping partisan interests out of it is a protection for both accuser and accused. It prevents us from being a participant in a seller's market—ready to believe some dirt for other reasons.

Let us set down two principles as we come to the rights of an accuser specifically. For our purposes here, we are assuming an accuser of established authority. If the accuser is in authority, then we do not have to worry much about their rights. The Sanhedrin accused Jesus, and at least as far as human judgment was concerned, they did not have to worry about retaliation. He was the Lamb led to slaughter. (Of course, we are leaving out of consideration here the days of vengeance that fell in AD 70.)

The first principle is that any accuser who is going to bring charges against those in authority over him, who could (if they wished) retaliate against him, must do his homework. We have already said this in the interests of justice. But an accuser in this position should have sheer self-interest in mind as well. If his evidence is compelling, then he should have it marshaled so that any who hear it are compelled to acknowledge that he is speaking the truth. More than that, all the principles we have referred to so far (two and three witnesses, non-anonymous witnesses on the record, and so on) are principles that protect the accuser. If they are absent, then everyone who looks at his charges can legitimately say, "This guy is a flake," and dismiss him. If these principles are absent, then absolutely anyone could make the same charges as well, whether they are true or false. So, if his evidence is slipshod, then the accuser either has a martyr complex, or he is attempting to try the case with sound bites in the rumor mill. He doesn't want his evidence sifted, he just wants bits of it to make it into the papers.

The second principle here is to remember that tyrannical establishments are not omniscient. However much they believe themselves to be godlike, they are not. This means that they cannot control every detail of what happens. For fallen creatures, bearing false witness is a task that no one is really up to. The false witnesses who were mustered against Jesus could not agree with one another, and everyone could see that they were conflicting witnesses. That kangaroo court was fumbling around and did not

have its act together, which is why the high priest decided
to stake everything on the words Jesus Himself said. The
same thing happened when the apostle Paul was being
accused before the Roman authorities in the latter part
of Acts. All Paul had to do was point out that assertions
by the authorities and proof from the authorities were
two different things. "Neither can they prove the things
whereof they now accuse me" (Acts 24:13).

　In short, being a stickler for the rules of evidence is a
much greater protection for the true underdog than it is
for those who are in authority. And when purported un-
derdogs are yelling that such rules of evidence are simply
supports for tyranny, they are giving their game away. A
true underdog knows who his true friends are. The biblical
principles of justice protect the accused and the accuser.

FROM A DISTANCE

So, what are some guidelines for sorting out situations
from a distance? You are not the judge, jury, or execution-
er, but you do read various blogs, and you see scandals and
gaffes processed on the evening news and in the paper.
What are you to do with some poor hapless soul who gets
himself into a local newsprint-and-ink bath? You are not
ever going to be asked to vote or determine anyone's fate.
You are just a small part of that great big ocean called
public opinion. Charges and countercharges fly, and once
the food fight is well underway, it is very difficult to determine who started it. Twitter has expanded the possibilities

so that with every public event we now can know how many tweets are favorable or unfavorable (as though this tells us anything about what is actually true).

David Bayly has offered this helpful advice:

> But when accusations and motives seem murky and you are not in the position of investigator or judge, one good way to know something about the truth of a situation is to examine the tactics of disputants. Tactics reveal truth.
>
> I don't mean we should look to see who speaks in saccharine tones or whose words drip ostentatious piety. I mean we should look at cold hard facts. Cold hard facts are these kinds of things: who went outside the local body first, who spread the dispute before the world? Who is accusing others of offenses against "what is written?" Who is charging others of offenses consisting primarily of tone and attitude? Who took their complaints to the Internet? Who tendered apologies? Who refused apologies?
>
> Such things are not conclusive. But they are indicative.[1]

As he says, such things are not conclusive. But they are more than enough to make you wary about asking a bad-reputation-monger to be a fishing buddy. So here are some slight variations on David's theme:

1. David Bayly, "The outernet," Baylyblog, http://baylyblog.com /blog/2006 /01/outernet (accessed March 27, 2015).

1. In the course of the controversy, who has offered various apologies, and who has not? Hint: the ones who have apologized and sought forgiveness in a number of settings are frequently the same ones who are accused of "never admitting they are wrong."

2. Who has refused to accept apologies? Hint: they are usually the same ones who are on a personal vituperation crusade in the name of love and unity.

3. Who took their complaints to the internet before they were properly adjudicated by the appropriate governing bodies? Who took the show on the road before the church had dealt with the issue? Everyone who is posting or running some variation of passingdogbytheears.com ought to withdraw their cybercharges and privately offer any legitimate evidence they might have to the right adjudicating bodies. Refusal to do so, as David points out, indicates something important.

4. Who believes that their personal feelings trump everything the Bible says about processing and handling evidence? It doesn't matter what the Scriptures say because they are the chief cook and bottle washer down at DeeplyGrieved.com.

5. David asked who is charging others with offenses that consist largely of "tone and attitude." Another way of making this point is to point out that some

charges require a deeply individualist interpretive grid, and others do not. Charging the church bookkeeper with embezzlement of $100,000 requires a commonly shared interpretive grid (the community's understanding of the difference between *meum* and *tuum*), the testimony of a couple of bank tellers, and some people on the elder board who can count. But watch out when the charge goes something like this: "And in the silence that followed the pastor's rebuke of my teenage son (poor baby), you could just feel the hostility radiate from the pastor, like heat from a stove." Really? You had the hate-o-meter out, did you? How fortunate. The people who make charges like this specialize in offering their own esoteric and individualist interpretation of the glance with a thousand meanings. And those who refuse to go along with their interpretation of others are clearly "loyal to a fault. Perhaps even a little cultish. So sad."

6. When the point of doing all this is recruitment, not justice, it is frequently taken as a personal affront when someone hears or reads what they say, but then reserves judgment until he knows more. But too bad. The Bible tells us to reserve judgment until we know (Prov. 18:17), and if someone is pushing us to disobey this clear requirement (or is busy explaining it all away), that tells you something.

7. Who is making claims that "a lot of other people have come to me," "or a lot of other people agree with me," but has also conveniently promised all those others that he would not mention their names?

8. And last, there is a common problem that David didn't touch on—but from his other comments, it is likely that he has seen this one too. This is the "You're So Vain You Probably Think This Song Is About You" problem. Once the conspiratorial mindset settles in, everything is interpreted as though it is directed at them personally—sermon topics, text selection, elder board decisions, lectionary readings, and blog posts. A favorite tactic of those who have fallen into this is a "just connect the dots" approach. Usually, quite a number of the dots they connect really have to do with other folks.

If a conscientious pastor encounters three husbands over the course of a month, say, who have an anger problem in their families, the congregation can expect to hear about this problem in the sermons. They will, of course, not hear any personal identifications ("And brethren, it is right that Mr. Smith is squirming in his seat just now . . . "), but they should hear about sins and difficulties that the pastor has good reason to expect are a problem in the congregation. One of the first rules of preaching is that you must never use the pulpit to settle personal scores. But another rule of preaching, just as important, is that you must never squander your time in the pulpit by thundering away at sins that never make their appearance in the lives of those gathered in front of you. And this is why we are writing now about justice. There are a number of people in our circles (in a number of situations) who clearly have no firm grasp of what justice is or how it functions. This is a common problem all over the country.

Spurgeon's "John Ploughman" wrote, "Last time I made a book I trod on some people's corns and bunions, and they wrote me angry letters, asking, 'Did you mean me?' This time, to save them the expense of a halfpenny card, I will begin my book by saying:

> Whether I please or whether I tease,
> I'll give you my honest mind;
> If the cap should fit, pray wear it a bit,
> If not, you can leave it behind.[2]

One more thing: pastors are often called into a dispute in an effort to recruit them to take sides, not to genuinely adjudicate and seek justice. Once again, "The first one to plead his cause seems right, until his neighbor comes and examines him" (Prov. 18:17). When he tries to slow things down, listen to all the evidence, and weigh the history, motives and facts of the case before rendering counsel, he is then accused of any number of failures.

2. C.H. Spurgeon, *John Ploughman's Pictures* (Pasadena, TX: Pilgrim Publications, 1974), 5–6.

ACCUSATIONS

From time to time we hear of some internet dust-up where charges are leveled against the pastor, session, or leadership of a Christian organization. The Bible is very explicit in the way it tells us to handle such circumstances. Therefore, when the charges are framed contrary to these biblical standards, they should simply be round-filed. For example:

1. The Bible prohibits anonymous accusation (Deut. 19), and because "John Smith" is not his real name, he does not have real biblical accountability in making his charges. A "male" in the "United States" needs to be narrowed down a bit further.

2. The Bible prohibits solitary accusation against elders (1 Tim. 5:19); this means that two or three (accountable) witnesses are required for each specification.

3. If anonymous accusers are allowed (see #1), then the requirement on #2 can be easily bypassed by a sole accuser (via multiple screen names of "George," "Stan," and "Melody," not to mention the always reliable "numerous sources have informed me"). This nameless cloud of witnesses all crossed their hearts and hoped to die.

4. A nameless individual does not get the same privileges that an honest man with a real name has. "John Smith" can't go vote that way, he can't get

a driver's license that way, and he does not carry his baptism that way. Does "John Smith" have a Christian name?

5. Two or three witnesses, when actually assembled and identified, must not have, by their previous misbehavior, impeached their credibility. But it is not uncommon to find that accusers have discredited themselves in previous internet food fights, and that the new "names" clustering around are identifying themselves by the company they keep.

6. If it is a substantive matter, a witness who testifies erroneously in one instance may be safely disregarded in his other testimony. "John Smith" testified one thing about what this church did to the poor Johnson family, and this was flatly contradicted by the Johnson family's public statement. The question that should therefore come to mind immediately is this: Are the other allegations of John Smith as reliable as this one was?

7. False witnesses need to have an outstanding memory; because they have to remember all the things they said previously, some of them pretty fruity. The truth is simple; the lie is complicated. The accusers of Jesus had no trouble rounding up the requisite number of witnesses, but they were still embarrassed by the manifest inconsistencies (Mark 14:59). The witnesses that come out of the

woodwork whenever something like this erupts on the internet are consistent in one thing only—their malice and envy.

8. In a biblical world, leaders (and others) do not have to prove their innocence. Their accusers have to prove their guilt, which is a manifestly different thing than merely asserting their guilt.

As we have watched various controversies on the web, driven by a spirit of accusation, we have not so much been disheartened at the various false accusers, gun-slingers, wannabes, thwarted aspiring sidekicks (have you seen *The Incredibles*?), and whatnot as we have been by the well-meaning Christians who have no grasp on the biblical principles for how to respond to this kind of thing.

APPEALING TO THE CHEAP SEATS

Another kind of allegation that pops up concerns public teaching or writing. This is not an allegation of personal wrongdoing that is denied by the accused and then needs to be proven. In that kind of situation, we need to have all the factors that we mentioned earlier—presumption of innocence, two or three witnesses, accountability for the accusers, and so on. But this is a different kind of allegation entirely, and evidence needs to be handled differently.

Not surprisingly, the Bible has something to say about public teaching, as well. Jesus was accused of promoting certain doctrines that His adversaries (for various reasons) twisted and misunderstood, and it is very interesting to note what the Lord's response to this was.

> The high priest then asked Jesus about His disciples and His doctrine. Jesus answered him, "I spoke openly to the world. I always taught in synagogues and in the temple, where the Jews always meet, and in secret I have said nothing. Why do you ask Me? Ask those who have heard Me what I said to them. Indeed they know what I said." And when He had said these things, one of the officers who stood by struck Jesus with the palm of his hand, saying, "Do You answer the high priest like that?" Jesus answered him, "If I have spoken evil, bear witness of the evil; but if well, why do you strike Me?" (John 18:19–23)

So the high priest asked Jesus about His followers, and he asked about His teaching. Jesus, in response to this "controlled environment" grilling, appealed to the cheap seats. He said, in effect, that His teaching ministry was public. He said that He taught these things in synagogues. He denied that He was involved in teaching anything in a clandestine way. Jesus then said that because of this He did not need to answer the question, and that the men who were interrogating Him needed to ask the general public what went down. "They know what I teach," Jesus said. The response to this was for one of the officers to strike Jesus and accuse Him of despising the lawfully constituted high priest. Jesus wasn't having any, and said, "If there is a problem with what I said, then what is it? And if there is not, then why did you hit me?"

Now let's stop for a moment. Given how words can be twisted and misunderstood, and certainly have been in many controversies, our point here is not that the accused is Jesus, and that the accusers are the Sadducees. Our point is simply a structural and juridical one. What was the nature of the charge? What was the nature of the (appropriate) response that Jesus gave? And where did the appeal go?

This kind of response—appealing to the public—is completely inappropriate if the charge against someone is that he murdered Smith on the evening of the thirteenth. In that kind of situation, you marshal the two or three credible witnesses and you evaluate and probe their testimony. The defense cannot get anywhere by producing ten witnesses who did not see him do it. An appeal to the crowd under such circumstances is demagoguery, not justice.

But when the charge concerns what someone has been teaching and saying in public, it is fully appropriate to appeal to that public, which is precisely what Jesus did in this situation. In many of these cases what the person is saying or teaching has been said or taught in many settings. We have read what they have written. For example, we have heard them explain to their critics their full commitment to the doctrinal system found in the Westminster Confession, face to face, in an unambiguous way. What the teacher has made available to the public in this setting is fully consistent with what we have heard him say in other places and times. In other words, the public has access to all the pertinent facts. If a judicial body is involved (e.g., a church court), then wait patiently for their response. The more people who are watching this, the better. This is a public event, and it concerns the public teaching of a public minister. This is a place where many people are involved in making sure justice is done. This is judicial transparency. The courts don't always get it right. Pilate had other forces pressing him (Luke 23:20–25). Thankfully, we know what Jesus actually taught.

FURTHER GUIDELINES CONCERNING ACCUSATIONS

We humbly offer these guidelines and counsel for anyone who receives bad reports against others, whoever they might be.

First, an accusation is not a conviction, but rather an opinion until proven with due process and by a legitimate authority (Matt. 18:15–2).

- "The first one to plead his cause seems right, until his neighbor comes and examines him" (Prov. 18:17).

- It is possible that the person(s) making the accusation could be holding back some of the facts of the case, or might have some axe to grind. If so, then we are not in a position to justly evaluate all the relevant information, and we simply do not know enough to make godly judgments.

Second, God has established civil, ecclesiastical, and familial authorities to make lawful judgments regarding the crimes and/or sins of others. Therefore, we should remember that many matters are simply none of our business.

- Such judgments are not left to individuals, though individuals might have their own private opinions in the matter.

- When individuals second-guess the judgments of the legitimate authorities, then publish their own judgments, they arrogantly exalt their private opinions over the wisdom of legitimate authorities.

- In legitimate courts there is a presumption of the innocence of the accused until proven guilty.

Third, proof must meet biblical standards.

- "One witness shall not rise against a man concerning any iniquity or any sin that he commits; by the mouth of two or three witnesses the matter shall be established. If a false witness rises against any man to testify against him of wrongdoing, then both men in the controversy shall stand before the LORD, before the priests and the judges who serve in those days. And the judges shall make careful inquiry, and indeed, if the witness is a false witness, who has testified falsely against his brother, then you shall do to him as he thought to have done to his brother; so you shall put away the evil from among you. And those who remain shall hear and fear, and hereafter they shall not again commit such evil among you" (Deut. 19:15–20).

- These witnesses must be accountable to the appropriate court and must be in a position whereby they can be cross-examined. Thus, anonymous accusations must be rejected as unsubstantiated and considered not credible.

- Not all witnesses are to be believed: "And two men, scoundrels, came in and sat before him; and the scoundrels witnessed against him, against Naboth . . . ." (1 Kings 21:13).

- Multiple credible witnesses are required before even receiving an accusation against an elder: "Do not receive an accusation against an elder except from two or three witnesses" (1 Tim. 5:19).

Fourth, those attempting to bypass legitimate authorities, and who spread accusations in order to harm those whom they accuse, are in sin, and their reports must not be received.

- Unproven accusations should not be published, since this would be, at best, gossip and, if driven by malicious motives, slander.

- "He who goes about as a slanderer reveals secrets, therefore do not associate with a gossip" (Prov. 20:19).

- "You shall not bear a false report; do not join your hand with a wicked man to be a malicious witness" (Exod. 23:1).

- "Whoever hides hatred has lying lips, and whoever spreads slander is a fool" (Prov. 10:18).

- "The simple believes every word, but the prudent considers well his steps. A wise man fears and departs from evil, but a fool rages and is self-confident. A quick-tempered man acts foolishly, and a man of wicked intentions is hated. The simple inherit folly, but the prudent are crowned with knowledge" (Prov. 14:15–18).

- "A fool has no delight in understanding, but in expressing his own heart . . . A fool's lips enter into contention, and his mouth calls for blows. A fool's mouth is his destruction, and his lips are the snare of his soul. The words of a talebearer are like tasty trifles, and they go down into the inmost body" (Prov. 18:2, 6–8).

- "It is honorable for a man to stop striving, since any fool can start a quarrel" (Prov. 20:3).

CHAPTER 5

CHARGES *and* LIES

Indeed, let God be true but every man a liar.
As it is written:
"That You may be justified in Your words,
and may overcome when You are judged."

ROMANS 3:4

When Christians collide with each other and get themselves into "sociological events" (i.e., conflicts), one of the first things to disappear is a sense of measured justice. When this happens, it is not the case that there is no sense of justice, because all the principles of justice can still be articulated, appealed to, and explained if the circumstance has to do with something that was done to *them*. The sin involved can be seen in the profound refusal to apply those same principles in the other direction.

The prophet says that God requires of us this: to do justice, to love mercy, and to walk humbly with Him. What does it mean to "do justly"? The Bible has a great deal to say about this, and we will start with one example that comes up a lot.

When someone else says something that you believe to be untrue, what do we call that? In time of conflict, it is the easiest thing in the world to call it a lie, and this makes the other person "a liar." When the traffic is going the other way, the choices aren't so simple. *Then* we call it the truth, or a mistake, or a difference in interpretation. And this means, applying the Golden Rule, that the latter is the standard we should apply to others, even to those others with whom we are in conflict. Or, as Leonardo da Vinci put it, "Do unto others as if you were the others."

A person is lying when two conditions exist. First, they are saying something that is untrue, and second, they know it to be untrue. If someone comes in and jokes that it is raining (because the sun is blazing hot) and yet someone inside who is a little gullible hears this and believes it, and then the second person goes down to the basement and tells someone there that it is raining, he is telling an untruth, but he is not telling a lie. The first person is telling a joke, not a lie. The second person is not lying because he honestly believes that what he is saying was true. The first person is not lying because his assumption is that everyone there will know the strict truth and take his manifestly untrue statement for what it is, a joke (although it's not funny once you have to explain it like that). Someone tells a lie when he says something untrue, knowing it to be untrue, and seeks to get others to believe it, although it is untrue.

This is not a difficult concept, and we all have it mastered . . . with regard to ourselves. If we made a mistake, an honest mistake, and passed it on to others, and we are subsequently charged with lying about it, we would all be able to parse the difference between intentional falsehoods and unintentional falsehoods. Moreover, we would demand that others observe the distinction as a matter of fundamental justice.

This is why it is a grave matter to charge someone with lying. If I make such an accusation, I am assuming upon myself the obligation to prove two things, not just one.

In a blog post, for example, we might charge someone with embracing and propagating a great number of false doctrines in his published books, and if we made the charge, we have the responsibility to set forth the arguments for making such an assertion. But at this point, judicially, nothing is settled. Those who have read our arguments and accepted them may take action on their own level, which would include things like not buying any more books by this author. But if, for some reason, this author were to show up at our church this coming Lord's Day, would we offer him the Lord's Supper? Absolutely, because he is judicially innocent until an appropriately adjudicatory body has found him guilty.

But there is still another level. In this example we have not accused the author of lying, because we do not know that he has been filling his books up with false statements knowing them to be false statements. In order to accuse him of lying, we would have to have either an ability to see hearts, which we do not have, or a "smoking gun" document that proves that the author knew he was making false statements. If we had an email to his publisher, for instance, in which he said that he was going to say that the Bible teaches x, y, and z although he knew good and well that it didn't, and we ascertained that the letter was genuine and not itself a fraud, then we would say that the author was teaching falsehood and that he was a liar. But short of that, we have absolutely no business making such a charge.

But we have to return for a moment to the question of seeing hearts. We can know (theologically) that all instances of error can be regarded as instances of lying to God. Self-deception is genuine deception, and, to a certain extent, we are all guilty of it. But this is not what is meant by saying that someone is "a liar." Scripture contains clear teaching on this distinction. The psalmist can say on the one hand that he was conceived in iniquity and that if God were to mark iniquities, he could not stand, and maintain on the other hand that he wanted God to judge and vindicate him because of his righteous behavior. The first is vertical (Godward), and the second is horizontal (manward). An elder is called to be blameless. This is one of the qualifications. But this has to mean blameless in the eyes of men—not guilty of rank hypocrisy, false living, deliberate deception, and so on. It cannot mean absolute blamelessness in the eyes of God, for then we would have no elders. Neither can it mean blamelessness because of the imputed righteousness of Jesus Christ, for then every Christian would be qualified to be an elder.

What this means practically is that when someone charges someone else with lying, they have assumed an enormous burden (whether they want to carry it or not). They must first demonstrate that the accused made false statements, and they must second demonstrate that they were made by a person who knew them to be false with intent to deceive. And it will not do to say that we do not need to make the case because the falsehood is all public record. Public records still need to be sifted, assembled, arranged, and the arguments presented. Suppose we had said that the author was a false teacher, and when asked why, we said simply that we did not need to answer the question because he "had written many books." We have frequently seen this sort of thing in "internet trials," where a man (or men) is accused of being a heretic. When asked for their "proof," the accusers point to a recording of a sermon or lecture. And if we were to take the next step and make the accusation that the author (above) was lying to us, we would be assuming a burden that should never be lightly assumed.

In the midst of any controversy, it is common for the rhetoric to increase and for the volume to be turned up. It is important, in these circumstances, that we take a couple of steps back and start asking some serious questions. Controversy requires caution and respect if we are to achieve true justice. There will always be a few self-appointed cru-saders—the keepers of the true flame—whose confidence exempts them from the need for careful investigation and handling of the facts. But for more cautious and respectful souls, an honest inquiry will be forthcoming.

Asserting something does not make it true. Just be-cause someone can see in his own mind how a person could reason from this point to that point (inference) does not make it a *necessary* inference. Being able to employ the imagination to conceive of how this or that doctrine could lead to some other dreaded doctrine, and then declaring that this is the inevitable outcome, is an exercise in both fantasy and false witness.

We have an obligation to love our brothers and our neighbors, and that means telling the truth about them. Malicious false witness violates the ninth commandment and inflicts serious damage on our neighbor. Negligent or careless false witness is also a breaking of the ninth com-mandment and can have similar effects. Our obligation is to honestly and accurately represent others when we disagree with them, not to assume that we know what they really meant. It does not take a big man to push over a straw man—little men are up to this simple task. Calvin warned against the refusal to hear contrary ideas by say-ing, "The less the interchange of opinion, the greater will be the danger of pernicious dogmatism."[1]

1. John Calvin, *Letters of John Calvin*, ed. Jules Bonnet (New York: Burt Franklin, 1972), 2:252.

We are commanded to love our enemies, and certainly we are to love our Christian brothers with whom we may disagree. Christians who hold different doctrinal views often fail this test. Personal pride and the desire to be right may override Christian character, and soon brother sins against brother. Too often we resort to anger, name-calling, mudslinging, questioning the sincerity or honesty of our brother, or other personal attacks. When this occurs, regardless of the theological strength of our arguments, we have lost—we have ceased to behave Christianly at that point. Biblical justice has the expectation that as we defend one truth of Scripture, we are not authorized to disregard the other truths.

Remember, this book has to do with public accusations and charges that are denied by the one accused. We are not talking about a conversation between friends, or between a husband and wife. If a wife were to ask her husband if he would mind not interrupting when their youngest daughter is trying to say something at the dinner table, only a churl would respond with demands for witnesses and tape recordings. Her observation might be "unjust" in a metaphorical sense, or it might be dead on, but in either case it should be resolved in a loving conversation, with both husband and wife speaking and listening, and taking things to heart.

But in a public setting, it is necessary for the accuser to be prepared to prove what he says. In order to do *that* (is this starting to sound familiar?), he must not be anonymous, he must be accountable to a body for his charges (in case they prove deliberate falsehoods), he must have independent confirmation of what he says (two or three witnesses). If these conditions do not pertain, a church body is prohibited by Scripture from entertaining the charges (1 Tim. 5:19). When authorities reject unsubstantiated charges, they are not covering anything up. They are being obedient.

In his fine book on the imprecatory psalms, John Day says, "This cry was the voice of the oppressed, the victim, the unjustly accused."[2] It is striking that he separated the "unjustly accused" from those who were oppressed or victims. And this starts an interesting train of thought. Consider King David. Before he was king, he was a favored one, and certainly the heir apparent. After he was king, he was, well, the king. We would not think of him as numbered among the class of the oppressed. Nor was he what we would call a victim (although his enemies tried to make him one). But was he ever unjustly accused? Yes, and often. The Psalms are full of his responses to such unjust accusations. This is important because oppression is usually a one-way street. The rich usually oppress the poor; the poor do not usually oppress the rich. But unjust accusations can go in any direction, and no one is immune from them. Not only so, but the Bible says that all are

2. John N. Day, *Crying for Justice: What the Psalms Teach Us About Mercy and Vengeance in an Age of Terrorism* (Grand Rapids: Kregel, 2005), 37.

to be protected against unjust charges. In fact, people in positions of authority are often a more inviting target. Because of this, the Bible insists that we have one standard of justice, period. But in our egalitarian era, it is too readily assumed that any charge against someone in authority cannot really be an unjust accusation.

"Thou shalt not raise a false report: put not thine hand with the wicked to be an unrighteous witness. Thou shalt not follow a multitude to do evil; neither shalt thou speak in a cause to decline after many to wrest judgment: Neither shalt thou countenance a poor man in his cause. If thou meet thine enemy's ox or his ass going astray, thou shalt surely bring it back to him again" (Exod. 23:1–4). We have here a wonderful biblical statement of justice: Lady Justice is blindfolded. She doesn't know if the accused before her is rich or poor, tall or short, black or white, elder or congregant. Note what it says in verse 3: "You must not countenance a poor man in his cause." Thou shalt not level the playing field. The question is not what outcome we might like. The issue is not whether an unjustly accused rich man can afford to be soaked just a little. In other words, you must not offer an accuser preferential treatment just because he is poor, or because he is accusing someone who is in authority. You must not grant the spilled-hot-coffee lawsuit against the restaurant chain just because they can afford it.

If someone accuses me of stealing something, I am within my rights to ask him to prove it or withdraw the charge. If I am innocent, I presumably know this, and so do not have to offer to "go pray about it." I already know the charge is baseless. If I go off to pray about it, that is not humility; it is playacting. If such a person says that he can prove it according to the biblical criteria, he comes and makes his charge before our elders (with me as pastor recusing myself). They check to see if he has independent confirmation, if he is accountable to a church body that will deal with him if he is lying, and if he is willing to use in public the name his mama gave him. If so, then he brings his charge, and both sides have the opportunity to cross-examine one another (Prov. 18:17).

But he might not want to bring a charge. And why not? Because he maintains that I have a bunch of levers under my desk that control the session of elders, and the whole thing would be hopeless. But this is not a good reason to not bring a charge; it is an additional unsubstantiated charge (against me and a number of godly men). This is like a man accusing me of stealing something, and when the session asks him to prove it, he thinks to deal with his lack of proof by saying that I actually stole two things. But for the life of me I cannot see how an unsubstantiated accusation of stealing a car can be proved by means of an unsubstantiated accusation of stealing two of them.

A little C.S. Lewis may be helpful. When Peter and Susan go to the old professor about Lucy's weird behavior, he gives them a basic lesson. Edmund was saying sane things, but his character was problematic. Lucy was saying crazy things, but she was a sane and honest person. The professor said, simply, that they should accept what she was saying and mind their own business. What she is saying can have only three possible causes—she is telling the truth, she is nuts, or she is deliberately lying. Peter and Susan testify that she is not a liar. It is plain as day that she is not nuts. Therefore, she must be telling the truth. "Bless me, what do they teach them in these schools?"[3]

This same trilemma comes out again in *Mere Christianity* when Lewis is dealing with the patronizing nonsense that wants to have Christ as a great moral figure in history, an ethical exemplar, but not the Son of God. The problem was that He claimed certain over the top things concerning Himself: "I am the Way, the Truth, and the Life." "No man comes to the Father except through Me." "I and the Father are one." "Before Abraham was, I am." If these claims were false, either He believed them, and was on the same level as a man who claims he is a poached egg, or He did not believe them, and was a monstrous charlatan. But if they were true, He was who He claimed to be. He is either the eternal Logos, or one of the worst specimens of a pretty bad humanity. But anyone can tell that the liar or lunatic options are not genuine options. He doesn't teach like a demagogue or like a basket of fruit. His moral character is compelling. He is Truth incarnate.[4]

3. C.S. Lewis, *The Lion, the Witch and the Wardrobe* (New York: HarperTrophy, 2000), 47–51, 189.
4. Lewis, *Mere Christianity*, 55–56.

To say that Truth is personal is the opposite of relativism. The Christian claim is that God was enfleshed and dwelt among us. We can certainly write true propositions about this on the classroom blackboard, but the propositions depend on the Person and not the other way around. In the most ultimate sense possible, Christians know that character matters.

Now one of the places where character matters is in the judges who have to sift through issues like this and weigh all the evidence. What are we to do with Bulverism,[5] for example (another observation from Lewis)? If you advance an argument, Bulverism undertakes to explain how you got so silly, instead of answering the argument. How does Lewis's correct rejection of Bulverism comport with his admirable support of Lucy's story about the wardrobe?

Godly men who know what justice is, what it smells like, and how it operates, have to accept the word of some witnesses and reject the word of others. One of the tasks confronting judges is to oversee a process in which false witnesses are impeached and true witnesses are confirmed. There are some very polished liars and some very inarticulate truth-tellers, and they both come before judges who are charged with dispensing wisdom and justice,

5. "Bulverism is a logical fallacy in which, rather than proving that an argument in favour of an opinion is wrong, a person instead assumes that the opinion is wrong, and then goes on to explain why the other person held it. It is essentially a circumstantial ad hominem argument. The term "Bulverism" was coined by C. S. Lewis." From "Bulverism," Omnilexica, accessed August 1, 2018, https://www.omnilexica.com/?q=bulverism.

sifting through real evidence and proofs (which do not lie), versus people, who sometimes do bear false witness (intentionally or otherwise).

Many things motivate witnesses to be false, and, as we saw in Chapter 1, envy has been the driving force of more than one trial, including those of Jesus and St. Paul (Matt. 27:18; Acts 13:45 and 17:5). Now why do the scriptural writers bring up envy? Isn't this Bulverism? No, because it is the true explanation of what is happening. But there are other instances where envy is not relevant in the same way. Suppose there are two scientists competing to unlock the secret of something. One of them is consumed with envy of the other one and mutters to himself every day as he goes to work. His envy makes him go to his lab earlier and stay later. He works harder, driven by bitterness, resentment and raw envy. As it turns out, this pays off, and he makes the discovery first and publishes his results first. And as far as the science goes, everything was fair and square. God will deal with his envy (because it is always relevant at some level), but those who read his journal article and reproduce his experiments (getting the same results) have confirmed his work and have shown that the envy is extraneous to the process—it can in principle be detached from the science. If hate-filled secularists affirm that the sun rises in the east, I don't have to deny it just to keep my soul pure.

But suppose the envious scientist has one of his grad students change universities to go study under the rival.

And suppose that, three months later, she charges the rival with sexual harassment, put up to it by the envious one. Now is the issue of envy relevant to the charges? Absolutely—not only is it relevant, it is necessary for the judges to consider it if they want to understand what has happened.

For example, in Moscow, Idaho, we had a potpourri bowl of charges leveled against us from "concerned citizens." One of them was the repeated charge that New St. Andrews College was out of compliance with Moscow zoning laws. Certain "objectivists" wanted to pretend that this was only about "the code," and that officials should only evaluate the code. That way, they would be "objective." This is not objectivity, it is cluelessness. By an insistence that the discussion be limited to this, they were in effect insisting that they were refusing to understand the situation. The complaint was filed by three individuals, each one of whom had a history with our church and/or the college.

Persons bring charges. Persons have motivations. Those motivations need to be evaluated, just like the charges do. No one is suggesting that we look at motivation only, and ignore the objective evidence. It is simply that persons cannot be extricated from charges; the whole thing cannot be turned into a math problem. Attempts to turn it into a math problem constitute a flight away from the basic Christian story. Christ stood before Pilate, who famously said, "What is truth?" When he asked this, Truth was standing right in front of him. Various robed falsehoods had arraigned Him, consumed with their envy. Pilate even saw the personal nature of the lies, but faltered when it came to understanding the personal nature of the Truth. Truth has ten toes. Truth was unjustly flogged by the provincial governor. Ultimate Truth had a crown of thorns jammed on His head. And Truth, when He appeared among us, caused various incarnate and envious lies to cook up some false charges, for personal reasons.

CHAPTER 6

THE USE *of* EVIDENCE

The first one to plead his cause seems right,
until his neighbor comes and examines him.

PROVERBS 18:17

We must always be on the side of justice, but until justice has been determined by an appropriate hearing under an appropriate jurisdiction considering appropriate evidence, we are required to reserve judgment. We might think someone is guilty, but our opinion, weak or strong, is not the same thing as evidence. The presumption of innocence is a biblical notion, and without credible witnesses (i.e., evidence), we may not assume that because someone is accused of a horrible act, the accusation is sufficient in itself to draw a just conclusion. Good rules of evidence are designed to promote justice. Some evidence is allowed, like eyewitness testimony, while other evidence is excluded, like hearsay reports. Once the credible evidence is on the table we still have the important task of interpreting that evidence in an appropriate context and with sound rules in place.

There must be partiality in judgment, but the partiality is always toward God's standards of justice. There really are evil people and bad actors, and God's law stands opposed to such persons. Nevertheless, their guilt needs to be established prior to the verdict being delivered. Careful attention to the evidence must be given before a sentence is made. Judges make judgments, but just judges always regard the law first, and the rules of evidence are a part of that law. It is all too common for people to rush to judgment when they are in no position to know or evaluate all the evidence. A personal hunch is not capable of delivering justice and it is fully capable of doing an injustice.

Newspaper reports, internet blather, and other types of rumor mills are not reliable evidence. It is possible to be in possession of two percent of the evidence but to assume that you are in possession of it all. For genuine justice to be rendered, all the available evidence, the right kind of evidence, the proper interpretation of the evidence and wise judges are all necessary. Our brains want to fill in missing information and will frequently do so rather than acknowledge that we simply do not know. We often assume actions, motives, and reasons not in evidence. Reading between the lines is dangerous and prone to produce injustice.

Moreover, repeating bad evidence is not evidence. The fact that two people are convinced that someone is guilty does not make that person guilty, and he is no guiltier if ten people are convinced, and post it on Facebook, and get a hundred and twenty-seven likes. Quantity cannot substitute for quality. To assert that a certain person, organization or company is guilty or evil does not make it so. Neither does the repetition of such statements prove the guilt of the accused. However, it might well indict the repeater of unsubstantiated reports for false witness.

TIE GOES TO THE RUNNER

We begin to unpack this with a couple of jokes that you may have heard before. They are offered not so much for the joke value as for what they illustrate about the power of interpretive grids, which (by the way) is the point of this chapter.

There was a guy who was convinced that he was actually a dead man, and so he went to a shrink. The psychiatrist had seen this kind of thing before, and so he decided not to take the direct approach. He therefore spent multiple sessions convincing his patient that dead men don't bleed. They read medical articles together, paid a visit to the morgue, and pretty much covered the subject. After many weeks, the patient was as convinced as a man can be that dead men don't bleed. So when the time was right, the shrink reached over with a pin, and quickly pricked the patient on the thumb. A bead of blood quickly formed, and the patient's face turned ashen white. "Dead men bleed after all!" he cried.

There was this other guy, impossible to please. He was critical of everything his friends did. Criticized their

trucks, their houses, their shotguns (they were duck hunt-
ers), and their hunting techniques. One day, to the joy of
his friends, one of them bought a dog who knew how to
walk on water. "This'll get him," was the general consen-
sus. The next Saturday, they all went duck hunting together, and spent their usual time in the duck blind listening to
their critical friend talk down about the coffee, the sand-
wiches they had, and the weather, not to mention everything else. But finally some ducks flew over, and one of the
men got a good shot, and a duck fell into the water. With
that, the magic dog ran out across the surface of the water,
deftly picked up the duck, and ran back to the blind. To
the astonishment of everyone there, the critical man said
nothing. Absolutely nothing. After half an hour, some
more ducks flew over and the same thing happened. Still
the man said nothing. Finally, one of the others, unable to
contain himself, asked, "So, did you notice anything about
the dog?" "Well," the man replied, "I didn't want to say
anything because I don't like being critical. But it looks to
me like your stupid dog can't swim."

This kind of thing is the result of an interpretive grid,
or paradigm. That grid is used to sort the information and
arrange the facts. It is not the case that facts simply arrange or interpret themselves. The facts do speak, but they
are not heard without an interpretive grid. All purported
facts, documents, truths, etc. are arranged into a narrative
by everyone who seeks to understand them. That narrative
will do justice to the facts or it will not, but the narrative is

not insignificant. Moreover, the narrative is always there. That narrative is what makes up the interpretive grid.

When I was a boy, I used to enjoy an elementary school writing exercise that was to take the list of new vocabulary words and use them all in a story or paragraph. If a teacher saw the same story come in from two different kids, this would be grounds for suspecting that one had copied from the other—and not grounds for thinking that this was "the only story" in which these words could appear. It is not that hard for the same words to appear in different stories.

All this is said because this particular issue is a point of stumbling for many who are trying to sort out claims and counterclaims, accusations and defenses. The undisputed facts of the case are like the vocabulary words, and different people with different agendas will write a different story around those "words." And the story they tell might even be consistent (for a time) with a limited list of the facts.

Take the undisputed facts as something like this: 1) Jim broke his neighbor's window, 2) half an hour later Jim was arrested by the police, and 3) Jim's wife bailed him out later in the evening.

This could result in something like this:

> Jim had been quarreling with his neighbor for some
> time over the neighbor's refusal to pay for a window
> in Jim's house that the neighbor's kid had broken the

week before. Finally, in exasperation, *Jim broke his neighbor's window* in retaliation, and called it good. But instead of taking it as a reasonable settlement, Jim's neighbor called the cops, and despite vigorously trying to explain himself, *half an hour later Jim was arrested by the police.* His wife was off at a baby shower at the time, and she received the unpleasant phone call there. And so *Jim's wife bailed him out later in the evening.*

Or this:

Jim was walking home late one evening and noticed flames coming out of his neighbor's attic. He pounded on the front door and got no response. He saw their cars were all there, and so he decided to break a window. So *Jim broke his neighbor's window* and woke the family up. They called the fire department, which arrived quickly, with the police just after them. The police were interested because an arsonist had been operating in the area. In all the confusion, someone thought that Jim fit a description of the arsonist they had, and *half an hour later Jim was arrested by the police.* Jim's wife was not at home, so he spent a little while trying to contact her, which he eventually did. And so *Jim's wife bailed him out later in the evening."*

Now let us say that Jim had some enemies who wanted to get him. In order to do so, they should have to do more than simply tell the first story and offer proof of the particular facts in italics that fit within that story. Telling a story in which certain facts all fit is not the same thing as telling a story that fits all the facts. And proof of the facts in italics only is proof of both stories if it is proof of one. If my story is that Queen Elizabeth II is a space alien, and it is an undisputed fact that she denies it (which is just what a space alien in that position would do), I cannot prove that she is a space alien by proving her denial.

This principle is why Joshua and his men stumbled when they accepted the word of the men of Gibeon. The facts were worn out clothes, cracked wine skins, and crusty old bread. The facts (which were indisputable) were placed (quite reasonably) in a particular story by the Gibeonites, but that did not confirm the story. The facts were consistent with this story, but consistency with a story is not the same thing as confirmation of a story.

This is why the investigative judges in Deuteronomy 19 were required to weigh the evidence carefully. Weighing the evidence carefully means a number of things (many of which are covered in this book). Among those things that must be weighed are the competing stories. Not only must the facts of the case be established (by credible and accountable witnesses, with opportunities for cross-examination), but so must the competing stories be told by competent narrators, with opportunity for cross-examination. "The deceased was despondent and committed suicide." "No, the deceased told me just yesterday how much he loved life." The fact that the deceased is deceased does not confirm one story or the other, even though it is consistent with both stories.

Clever lies (or, to use Orwell's phrase, lunatic misunderstandings) are those which weave as many of the factual "vocabulary words" as possible into the narrative. It may even get to a point where you wonder if a competing narrative is even possible. But this is precisely why the narratives must be examined side by side, with both narrators fully accountable. This is also why, everything else being equal, the narrative of the accused is accepted at face value. This is the biblical basis for that great American principle of the tie going to the runner.

SINS ARE LIKE GRAPES

Sins are like grapes; they come in bunches. Observant people see this and have to deal with it, but it still has to be kept distinct from any judicial proceeding. Wise pastors see this also and are able to make connections between apparently disparate sins in the life of someone they are counseling. But providing pastoral counsel is not the same thing as bringing someone up on charges.

This can be a real trouble when someone who should be receiving pastoral help and counsel decides that the best defense is a good offense, and goes after those who could be helping him. When disgruntled church members attack the elders or the pastor, we are rarely dealing with an Athanasius standing up *contra mundum*. The pastor can see what is being done to him, and understands why, but he is still not in a position to explain it to the world.

Say that a parishioner has severe problems in his marriage and treats his wife like dirt. The pastor sees this and gets in his face about it. At this point, the one rebuked has different choices. First, he can repent, and receive the rebuke. Second, he can receive the rebuke on paper, but not really change. Third, he can just leave the church. Or fourth, he can get mad and counterattack. "How dare the pastor try to deal with my sins? Who does he think he is?" The counterattack can take, and frequently does take, the form of personal critiques of the pastor. And if the pastor is the kind of man who preaches and teaches against sin in the congregation, it is likely that the agitator can find some listening ears that have been boxed as well.

Now this means that the sin being committed against the pastor is not really the central sin. Often the debate gets sidetracked at this point. One person says not to slander the pastor, and the other person says it is not slander, every word of it being true. The whole thing gets discussed in those terms and the diversionary tactic has worked. The subject has been changed. We are no longer talking about the way this man treats his wife. Even if the person defending the pastor does so successfully, we are still not talking about how this guy treats his wife.

The pastor can see all this and still not be in a position to bring it up. One reason is pastoral confidentiality.

While pastoral confidentiality is not an absolute, it is still important to be as discreet as possible about things you discovered about a person's life while counseling them. It is not the case that if a counselee becomes an adversary that all bets are off. Second, the pastor needs to be on guard against possible ungodly motives of his own. Retaliation is the easiest thing in the world, and it would be better to keep things to yourself than to possibly give way to that very carnal impulse. Third, retaliation of this kind would frequently look like (because it would be) an *ad hominem* attack. Not everything that the pastor knows about someone is necessarily relevant to a dispute.

This is all granted. But pastorally, the relevance doesn't necessarily lie on the surface. Whether this man treats his wife like dirt and whether the pastor voted contrary to his session's instructions at General Assembly are logically distinct. But in congregational snarls they are often not distinct practically. Because Paul was a shrewd pastor if there ever was one, let's take a Pauline example.

At the end of 2 Corinthians, Paul was answering objections to his ministry—he was charged with all kinds of stuff. (The only reason St. Paul does not hold the record for attack blogs set up against him is that attack blogs hadn't been invented yet. But his enemies still did all right with the old technology.) The apostle Paul was thoroughly slandered by his opponents at Corinth. For just a couple examples, he was attacked for financial misbehavior (2 Cor. 12:16–17), and for writing powerful letters but being a real loser in person (2 Cor. 10:10). Now Paul knew exactly what was going on—he was a real pastor of souls. What did he expect to find in Corinth when he arrived there? "For I fear, when I come, I shall not find you such as I would, and that I shall be found unto you such as ye would not: lest there be debates, envyings, wraths, strifes, backbitings, whisperings, swellings, tumults" (2 Cor. 12:20). In short, when Paul overturned the big flat rock, he expected to find every kind of creepy-crawly under there. If this is the kind of sin that people are willing to commit, against an apostle, why not against a lowly pastor?

But the interesting thing is what Paul expresses a concern about: What did he think he would find as the root cause of the senseless debating, the acidic envying, the outbursts of anger, the unnecessary strife, the backstabbing, the whispering campaigns, the shameless and swelling self-promotion, and the tumults? All these are obvious sins, and so why not just call for repentance for these sins? Paul knew that these were symptomatic sins—the spots on the skin, not the disease.

In the next verse, he says this, "And lest, when I come again, my God will humble me among you, and that I shall bewail many which have sinned already, and have not repented of the uncleanness and fornication and lasciviousness which they have committed." Paul was expecting many of the saints at Corinth to have unresolved, unrepented sin in their sexual closets, and he saw this as the driving force behind the problems of verse 20.

If all the rules of evidence mean anything, they mean that the clear presence of one sin is not sufficient to convict someone of having committed another sin. But discipline and love in the church are to be more familial than juridical, and in organic settings, certain things go together. Parents need to understand this, as should pastors and elders. As God gives opportunity, the clear presence of one calls for sensitive probing (and not insensitive broadside accusations: To do that would put you in the category of people that the apostle Paul was worried about). James understood the same principle. "For where envying and strife is, there is confusion and every evil work" (Jas. 3:16). The Scriptures teach us that cultivated plants like envy, acrimony, and strife grow in the devil's hothouse. And the devil always grows other stuff too.

CHAPTER 7

WITNESSES

You shall not circulate a false report. Do not put your hand with the wicked to be an unrighteous witness. You shall not follow a crowd to do evil; nor shall you testify in a dispute so as to turn aside after many to pervert justice.

EXODUS 23:1–2

Not bearing false witness is fundamental to biblical justice, although it is possible to *deliberately* bear false witness or *carelessly* bear false witness. While there is a qualitative difference between perjury and a mistake, the unjust effects on the innocent are similar. Honest, careful, and faithful testimony is a necessity. As we have established, this requires the opportunity for cross-examination and corroboration (Deut. 19:15). This is set forth again in Matthew 18:15–46: "Moreover if your brother sins against you, go and tell him his fault between you and him alone. If he hears you, you have gained your brother. But if he will not hear, take with you one or two more, that `by the mouth of two or three witnesses every word may be established."[1] It is the burden of the accuser (or the prosecutor of the accusation) to prove guilt.

The importance of truthful, credible witnesses is seen in the Bible's strong sanctions against perjury. To bear false witness before God is a form of blasphemy, since God Himself is just and false witness offends that justice. The biblical penalties for perjury require that the false witness receive the same penalty that the accused would have received had he been found guilty, up to and including death.[2] A witness is prohibited from shading or exaggerating the truth in order to achieve a certain outcome. This is a perversion of justice. Scrupulous honesty is essential (Exod. 23:1–3).

Witnesses are sometimes tempted to spin the facts in a certain direction because they are "concerned" that someone they "know" to be guilty "might get away with it." Planting evidence becomes a way of helping the case reach a foregone conclusion, which is another way of perverting the justice process. This is often done on the informal level, taking things out of context and twisting words in support of an accusation. The apostle Peter

1. Also: "By the mouth of two or three witnesses every word shall be established" (2 Cor. 13:1). "Do not receive an accusation against an elder except from two or three witnesses" (1 Tim. 5:19). "Anyone who has rejected Moses' law dies without mercy on the testimony of two or three witnesses" (Heb. 10:28).

2. See Leviticus 19:12; Deuteronomy 17:6–7; 19:16–21; Proverbs 19:5, 9; 25:18; Matthew 19:18; Mark 10:19; Luke 18:20; Romans 13:9.

observed this kind of false witness being used against his fellow apostle, Paul, when he described how some persons dealt with Paul's teaching, saying, "which untaught and unstable people twist to their own destruction, as they do also the rest of the Scriptures" (2 Pet. 3:16). Not all witnesses are equal—witnesses must be tested before receiving their testimony into evidence. When they do testify they must "tell the truth, the whole truth, and nothing but the truth."

No situation is so clear cut that it cannot be murkified by those who have a motivation to do so. But motivation is not all that is needed. In order to get away with this kind of thing, there usually has to be some kind of support group, some kind of amen corner. This serves as a form of emotional reinforcement and is done in lieu of seeking out actual accountability. A man makes a series of charges which need to be proven, and if he doesn't have proof, he has a problem. So instead of hanging out with the skeptical, he has to seek out a group that will not require him to prove anything because what he has said is "obvious" to all of *them*. The thing that unites them is not a truth that has been established in accordance with Scripture; it is simply a grievance plank in their party platform.

Those who begin to operate this way have introduced raw partisanship into community, and they show that they do not know how to live in community. All communities have to deal with the reality of sin, and for churches this would include the sins that might occur anywhere—sin in the leadership, sin in the congregation, sin in the choir, or sin in the youth group. This would include sins of browbeating and tyranny from the leadership and backbiting and false accusation against the leadership. Things can go wrong anywhere. Because of this, Christian communities have been given the tools to deal with sin. When a body does not have the means of fighting off sin (moral infection), that particular body has AIDS: the immune system is shot. This was why discipline was so important to the Reformers.

But not only must a body fight off infection, it must fight off *the right one*. More than one ailment creates a situation in the body where the thing that feels like it must be done is the very thing that you must not do. You feel like scratching, but you must not. You feel like you must drink water, but you must not. You feel like you are freezing, but you must not heap up the blankets. When it comes to diagnosis and treatment, feelings are not authoritative. In fact, feelings are frequently 180 degrees off of authoritative.

But these feelings can still be insistent, imperious. A person feels that if he doesn't act, then all is lost. But here is where God's requirement of two or three witnesses comes in. This is not a blind bureaucratic process instituted by the Holy Spirit for inscrutable reasons. This is, to continue the medical metaphor, simply prudence: Before you amputate a leg, *you must get a second opinion*. And if there is any remaining doubt at all, you must get a third opinion. This is because cutting up the body, or chemotherapy, or radiation therapy, is a big deal, and you don't just do it because somebody feels like it.

"Two or three witnesses" is the ancestor to our civil standard which says that before someone can be pronounced guilty, he must have been found guilty "beyond all reasonable doubt" by twelve people, selected at random, who have been required to hear both sides of the case in detail, with each side forced to submit to cross-examination from the other side. Our civil justice system has many problems that have crept into it and corruptions that must be dealt with. But when it comes to adhering to the basic concepts of justice, most (vestigially biblical) civil courts have a far better grasp of justice than do vigilante accusers in the church.

WITNESSES AND PROCESS

Matthew 18 is not talking about what many people assume it is talking about. Jesus is talking about one application of the biblical principles of justice; He is not talking about all of them. Not even close. This text is often taken in a wooden manner and fails to recognize that wisdom always requires much more than a procedural checklist. All the biblical principles of justice come into play.

The situation Jesus describes is limited to someone who sinned against you, not someone who sinned generally. For example, if you saw someone from the church shoplifting at the mall, Matthew 18 does not, strictly speaking, apply. The central principles still apply, but the sin was not "against you." Moreover, the witnesses who are brought (in Matthew 18) are not witnesses of the original offense; they are merely witnesses of the second confrontation. If the person refuses to hear it, then the accusation is brought to the church. Further, there is no assumption that the elders of the church are involved in this before it gets to the level of the entire church, though as shepherds, they might come alongside to help guide the process.

So we misunderstand Matthew 18 if we try to make it the template for every form of church discipline. It is the template for one kind of situation calling for church discipline. And this does not remove the need for two or three witnesses in all forms of church discipline. The requirement is an ancient one for God's people, going back over a thousand years before this particular application of it by Christ.

This fundamental principle of the Old Testament is carried over into the New, and not just in Matthew 18: "This is the third time I am coming to you. In the mouth of two or three witnesses shall every word be established" (2 Cor. 13:1). And "Against an elder receive not an accusation, but before two or three witnesses" (1 Tim. 5:19).

So what is Jesus talking about in Matthew 18? What Jesus is talking about could include what in modern parlance would be called an intervention. The fact that Jesus stipulates that there has been a sin against the person who initiates everything means that he has "standing" to be there. Let us say that there is a man who drinks way too much, and everyone who knows him knows about it. He is putting away a couple six packs a night. One person goes to him about his drinking problem. If he hears that person (as he ought to do), then that person has gained a brother. But if he refuses to hear it, then the first person to confront him ups the ante, taking two or three witnesses—witnesses of the reception (or lack of reception) of a well-deserved admonition or rebuke.

And of course, the passage applies straight across when there has only been one significant sin, as with a business deal gone wrong, or marital infidelity.

Now suppose it is an intervention over an issue that is perhaps culpable, but far less serious. Let us say that the recipient of the Matthew 18 visits is someone who does not ask for paper bags at the supermarket, even though his wife has told him that she is trying to save them. He keeps bringing home the plastic ones. He keeps forgetting. Is this something that you want to start such a process over? Is this something that should end by "telling it to the church"? Of course not, not unless you want the whole church staring in disbelief at the accusers who brought the charge. "And so, we tried warning our brother, but he wouldn't take us seriously." I dare say.

Jesus is talking about resolution of personal problems between individuals, and it is clear that He is talking about serious problems, the factualness of which is not disputed, or which cannot be disputed. "Somebody is drinking a couple of six-packs every night, and it isn't me. Everyone who knows us, knows this."

Moreover, since "love covers a multitude of sins," not every personal offense requires a Matthew 18 process. Some things should be covered (which is not the same thing as covering up a sin). In some matters, we might follow Matthew 18, but without sufficient evidence to prove an offense, we might need to drop it and take the process no further.

So where should we look in Scripture when someone is accused of committing a particular crime or sin, and he disputes it? He says he wasn't there; he was on the east coast at the time the murder occurred. Suppose that someone accuses someone else of lying about something, and the one accused says that he was not lying. Now what? When the claim is legitimately and reasonably contested, what passages do we look to? Clearly, whatever process we adopt, the passages from Deuteronomy apply. And from Corinthians. And from 1 Timothy. Otherwise, the process of accusation becomes the ultimate weapon—a weapon which false witnesses are willing to use, given their willingness to sit loose to the truth. In such a battle, godly Christians are restrained in their responses, unwilling to fight dirty as they fight back. But in some instances, they might be provoked into fighting dirty in a hypothetical way, simply in order to make a point. "The person who is accusing me in this situation is doing it because he found out that I knew he is wanted for child molestation in three states. That is why . . . excuse me? I have to prove that? Oh. Never mind."

If the testimony of just one man will be received when the charge is denied by the accused, those who are willing to receive it are well out of the biblical realm and into a realm worthy of Lewis Carroll. In fact, people who are willing to receive one witness like this are so far gone that they will no doubt receive (and defend) the testimony of anonymous accusers as well. Since the accused is "a tyrant," well, of course, the witnesses have to be anonymous because they are afraid of the tyrant. Verdict first, trial afterwards. Ready, fire, aim! But of course, when disobedience is an emotional necessity, excuses are always available.

Another common expectation of some witnesses is the demand that their word is sufficient to prove the case. A parent or pastor or policeman or judge is told that this is the way it all happened, and the witness expects that their testimony should settle the matter. "I told you what happened. Why don't you believe me? I'm an honest person, so why won't you take my word for it?" The Bible requires that the testimony of even the best witness—*the* most credible witness—must be corroborated. That is the reason the scriptural requirement is two or three witnesses.

Now think for a moment. What is meant by two or three? Which is it? Does God want us to have two witnesses, or three witnesses? Which is the minimum? Well, life being what it is, the answer is, it depends. This is why,

in dealing with charges made against anyone, one of the
first things that judicious elders should do is divide the
witnesses into two categories. The categories are "those
who are personally involved" and "bystanders."

The testimony of a bystander would go something
like this: "Yes, on the evening of April 13, I saw our small
group Bible study leader stagger out of the bar with a
hoochie-mama on his arm. My wife and I were down-
town in order to see a movie, and just happened across
him. He seemed surprised." The bystander happens to
be a witness of something, and if this something is independently confirmed by another person from the church
who was down there to see the same movie, it appears that
you have the requisite two witnesses. Neither witness has
a dog in any fight—they are simply there and can confirm
or deny what is alleged.

But suppose the witness does have a dog in the fight,
and suppose the judicial mechanism is one of the weapons
he picks up to advance that fight? How many witnesses do you need now? Suppose Mr. Martin is exceedingly
peeved that he was not hired to be the choir director. And
suppose further that reports start mysteriously circulating
in the church that the new Scoundrel Choir Director has
been seen out late with various hoochie-mamas. Who can
verify this? Steps forward Mrs. Martin to confirm, with
grief in her heart, that the charges are, alas, true. And after
she saw it with her own eyes, she came right home and
told Mr. Martin about it. And Mr. Martin has supplied

us with a signed affidavit, solemnly averring that this is in fact what Mrs. Martin told him (and, of course, he can testify that Mrs. Martin is a very honest person). The concept that some people have of justice is enough to make a cat laugh.

So if the testimony is bogus or contradictory, it doesn't matter how much you multiply it. Did the Pharisees have more than two or three witnesses who were willing to say that they heard Jesus say He was going to destroy the Temple? Sure thing. The numerical requirements are easy enough to meet, especially if you have access to a copy machine. But the Bible does not require us just to hear the charges and then count the noses of those making them. The Scriptures require that the judges hearing the charges make diligent inquiry (Deut. 19:18). And in making diligent inquiry, it is a matter of interest to everyone whether or not the charges are being brought by a man's enemies. In other words, sound judgment requires wisdom, and wisdom requires the ability to see three-dimensionally.

A bystander witness is simply discharging a civic or ecclesiastical obligation—testifying to what he saw. He happened to be there, and he can tell us what he saw there. An adversarial witness will use evidence so long as it is doing what he wants it to do, and then when the charge doesn't work anymore, he drops it like a hot rock. But it is still amazing how long they will cling to a story after its usefulness to them has, um, diminished.

So there are witnesses, and there are witnesses. And always beware of cyberwitnesses who are carrying a grudge and who will not submit to cross-examination. This is the kind of witness who can be caught out, dead to rights, and still manage to say, "Who are you going to believe? Me or your lying eyes?"

SELF-INCRIMINATION

The requirement of independent confirmation is not waived simply because a person confesses to something. That independent confirmation may certainly be circumstantial, but authorities in any realm ought to be wary of simply accepting someone's accusation against himself.

Say that a man, wracked with guilt, goes to the police and confesses to having murdered someone the year before. The details of his story still have to be checked out, and the rules of evidence still have to be remembered while doing it. If he shows the police where the body is buried, and it becomes independently clear that this confession is accurate, then he can and should be charged. But if the only thing to go on is the confession, then it is not good enough. Why is this?

There are a number of reasons, and the thought behind the well-known action of "pleading the Fifth" is a thoroughly biblical one. The Fifth Amendment allows us (in the civil realm) to refrain from making any statements that might tend to incriminate us, and it holds further that we may therefore remain silent without that silence being used as evidence of guilt. Why is this a scriptural principle? Or, better stated, why is this a healthy reflection of a biblical principle?

In the civil realm, a man can be worked over with rubber hoses until he decides that ten years in the Big House would be preferable to the treatment he is getting. Other kinds of browbeating, coercion, and manipulation have been known to produce "confessions." If we allow a simple confession to suffice for conviction, and nothing confessed has to line up with the way things are in the external world, then we have opened the door to thumbscrews. This was not an academic worry for our founding fathers, and neither is it an academic worry today.

What about in the church? There are churches where the rubber hoses are not made out of rubber, but they still work pretty well. All sorts of pressures can be brought to bear on someone under authority, and one of the central protections for the individual is a corporate and institutionalized understanding (on the part of everyone) that a solitary confession is not enough to convict anyone of anything. To simply allow people to come forward as their own accusers (and to require nothing more) is to affirm the Stalinist show trials as textbook models of justice. And even if we take away the capacity for physical coercion that Stalin had, the ecclesiastical world is not lacking men like Diotrephes, who loved to have the preeminence (3 John 9), or elders who neglect Peter's admonition (1 Pet. 5:3) and lord it over the flock. Jesus thought that power-manipulation was going to be enough of a temptation in the church that He explicitly warned His disciples against ruling the way pagan civil rulers did. Tyrants in any realm can always say, "Vee haff vays . . ." And they do. This is why maintaining tight views of what constitutes justice (in every direction) is so essential for life together. Without it, everything tumbles into genuine fears and weird paranoias.

There are other reasons to be wary about self-incrimination in the church, even in the absence of authoritarianism. People confess to things for different reasons, and in various states of mind. Suppose someone confesses to a particular sin, but they do so while in the throes of a black depression. Should the pastor or elders simply take the confession and proceed as though it was necessarily true? Suppose someone very manipulable is in a relationship with someone very manipulative. Say the husband is unfaithful, yet he has his wife so browbeaten that she blames herself for his infidelity. Will her confession of her responsibilities be an accurate assessment of the situation? Almost certainly not.

There are any number of ways that problems like this could develop. Suppose the confession is taken out of context and placed in a different setting entirely. Say that a husband with a sensitive conscience goes to the grocery store to buy a loaf of bread. While standing in the checkout line, he notices the lady on the front of *Cosmopolitan* acting like a sale at Dillard's—forty percent off. And let us say that he does more than notice her—he gives way to unbridled lust. But by the time he gets out to his car, his senses come back to him, and he is overwhelmed with remorse. He then gets home and confesses "infidelity" to his wife. Now presumably he explained the context to her, and exactly what it is he is confessing to. But he knows that Jesus taught that lust in the heart is equivalent to adultery, and so he confesses it in that way. He broke the seventh commandment. Later in the evening, he follows this up with a note written in a card, seeking forgiveness again for his "infidelity."

Now all this is fine, so long as neither he nor his wife are obsessing about it (which people with sensitive consciences frequently do, incidentally). But suppose the wife takes the note he wrote down to the pastor, shows it to him, and wants to know if the church will allow her to divorce her husband. There it is, in black and white. He came as his own accuser, confessed to having broken the seventh commandment, and is guilty of infidelity. And Jesus taught that infidelity is one of the few scriptural grounds for divorce. So, can she have a divorce? No.

Faithful Christians (particularly faithful Christians who have read some of the Puritans) frequently confess sin in a robust way, pushing their confession into all the nooks and crannies identified by the Westminster Larger Catechism. But to take a confession from one context and place it in another context (e.g., from a note of apology to divorce court) without bringing in all the other principles of justice is negligence at best and gross injustice at worst. Once again, wisdom must look behind the curtain before rendering a judgment.

This is simply because when the man apologized for sin X, he was not seeking forgiveness for sin Y. This would become immediately apparent if the principle of Proverbs 18:17 were remembered, and poof, there go the grounds of divorce. This mistake is a variant of the fallacy of equivocation, where the meaning of the terms changes in the middle of the argument: "God is love. Love is blind. Ray Charles is blind. Therefore . . ." But in this case the meaning of words and phrases is changed by placing them in a different context.

When men want justice, they must deliberate. They must go slowly. They must sleep on it. They must ask questions and allow those who differ with them to ask their questions as well. They must be eager for this and not resent it. And until there is overwhelming evidence, checked, cross-checked, and tied down with baling wire, the accused didn't do anything wrong. This is what is meant by "innocent until proven guilty beyond a reasonable doubt." A man should not be convicted unless the evidence requires it beyond a reasonable doubt, when considered by reasonable people. And reasonable people are defined by Scripture and not their own assessments of their own wisdom.

None of this prevents a guilty person from confessing their sins or crimes and then promptly providing the corroborating witnesses and evidence to support their confession. It is not that they cannot confess—they should confess if they are guilty. Rather, it is necessary that their confession be verified by other evidence. A repentant person will confess their sins and crimes readily and not try to see what they can get away with, or hire the best lawyer to see if they can get off. A guilty man would say to the police, "I'm turning myself in because I murdered my neighbor. You can find the body in the basement and the gun under my bed. How else can I help with your investigation?" Or, "Pastor, I did commit adultery. Her name is Delilah Jones, and the clerk at the Sleazy Arms Hotel can verify that we met there every Thursday night for the last six months. Will you go with me to confess to my wife?"

CHAPTER 8

IMPUTING MOTIVES
and JUSTICE

You shall not hate your brother in your heart. You shall
surely rebuke your neighbor, and not bear sin because of him.
You shall not take vengeance, nor bear any grudge against
the children of your people, but you shall love your neighbor
as yourself: I am the LORD.

LEVITICUS 19:17–18

Mysteries beg to be solved and, therefore, when one presents itself, our minds go on a mission to explain it. When the resolution is not plainly evident, our brains often attempt to fill in the gaps. Something was done or said, and the only interpretation we can come up with that makes any sense (to us) is that they *must have intended* to embarrass, seduce, tempt, twist, manipulate, or otherwise make our lives miserable. We have some of the story, but we feel compelled to read between the lines. Nevertheless, the blank space between the lines is *blank*, and thus the interpreter's imagination tends to fill it in and create a fiction. The temptation to spin a story in our own favor and in opposition to an antagonist is great. God alone is the searcher and knower of hearts. Motives can be known only if they are revealed by the evidence and not by mere speculation or imputation.

The Bible teaches that there are both good and evil hearts, and that these hearts produce different kinds of behavior. Moreover, words themselves are a type of behavior, and they can and do reveal the kind of heart that produced them. Therefore, behavior certainly might be an indicator of motives. Nevertheless, good intentions can also pave the way to the bad place. A gossip might intend no harm, yet still unjustly damage a reputation. Both carelessness and malice (as well as many other sins) could lead to the sin of gossip. Malice, envy, and hate are separate sins that are harder to get at than, say, the sin or crime of false witness. And even those require their own credible evidence before justice can be rendered.

It is a valuable lesson to learn to refrain from judging the motives of others. This is a blessing beyond compare when it comes to cultivating a healthy marriage and family, and it is oil on troubled waters in many relational conflicts. But it is not an all-purpose cure-all. The apostle Paul said that as far as it concerned us, we were to be at peace with all men. But sometimes the other party does not cooperate, and you cannot be at peace with them. A refusal to impute motives does not automatically fix everything—but frequently it is a great help in not making things worse.

What is it to impute motives? I am judging the motives of others when I not only accuse them of wrongdoing, but I also publicly declare the internal heart reasons they had for doing it. If I see a man hop into my car and drive off in it, I can know that he stole my car. But what I don't know is why. If I go down to the police station and report that so-and-so stole my car out of envy, I am judging motives. And this is something that is beyond my competence to judge. I don't know that, and if all I have seen is the back of his head, I can't know it. A man could have many motives (unknowable by me) for stealing my car. It could just be his chop-shop job, it could be greed, it could be envy, it could be fear. I don't know.

But this is not true when I know the other person very well, or if I know him reasonably well and have talked to him a great deal. "I will never forgive you for cheating me out of my share of the inheritance," says one sister to another. Now the second sister knows the motivation for all her sister's subsequent behavior, and she knows it without imputing motives.

Imputing motives in the destructive sense happens this way: a woman hears her husband answer her questions with monosyllables only. She knows that if she answered him that way it would be because she was ticked off at him, and since he is answering her that way, he must be resenting her. But this is not true. He is answering her this way because he is a blockhead. And she has a worse situation because she imputed motives—she is dealing with what she thinks is malice when she ought to be dealing with stupidity.

The motives of others can be known, but not through what we might call great experiments in telepathy. We cannot peer into the heart of another and figure out what is going on there. But we can listen and hear, and ponder and know. If someone tells you what his plans are, and then systematically goes about implementing them, then it is not hubris to think you know what is happening.

There are at least two motives (one good and one bad) for trying to figure out the motives of others.

The bad one first: When someone has wronged you, a very natural and carnal response is to want to strike back. "You're a thief!" doesn't seem to cut it. Presumably he knows that already. But "You're a thief who stole my car to make up for your vast and profound feelings of inferiority compared to people like me!" has a real punch to it, although he might not hear the last part since he already turned the corner and your muffler has a hole in it. This is one of the reasons people come up with motives when they don't really know them. It makes it easier to condemn with turbocharged enthusiasm, and those who want to retaliate against others with value-added condemnation are forgetting the Lord's extensive teaching on this subject. William F. Buckley said somewhere that intellectual probity can be seen not only in what a man says and does, but also in what he puts up with from others. The sinful desire for vengeance is one of the driving forces that tempts us to see motives in others that we cannot really see. Seeing that motive inspires us to strike back harder. When we have been wronged, it is rare that we come up with exculpatory motives for the offender. "He probably stole my car because his wouldn't start, and his wife must be in labor, and he had to get her to the hospital, and I didn't answer the door fast enough." So, the motives for our attributing motives to others are relevant.

But another reason for dealing with motives is pastoral. One of the reasons for trying to figure out why a person is doing what he is doing is in order to be able to help him. Did a man commit adultery against his wife because of good old-fashioned lust? Because he was starved for respect, and this other woman offered him a counterfeit and flattering version of it? Because he was in a desperate situation in his marriage and he wanted to do something drastic to blow it up, something that would make his wife divorce him? Motives matter, and pastors are trained to draw them out. And sometimes it is not necessary to draw them out—the motives are lying right on the surface of virtually everything the person says in a counseling session. One man may find himself in constant conflicts with his neighbors because he is a belligerent gorilla. Another man may be in the same position of constant conflict because he is drastically insecure and he is trying to compensate for it. Another man may be appointed by God as the Tishbite on his block, and so he goes around rebuking abominations, confident that he is doing the will of God.

Motives vary, and motives matter. But motives cannot just be grabbed out of the air and randomly assigned to people.

In various controversies we face, it is not uncommon for the motives of some of the antagonists to be almost a complete mystery. We couldn't presume to say anything about their motives, because we have no earthly idea what they are. But with other adversaries, we have a pretty good idea of what is driving them, and we know this because we know them, and have talked to them at great length, and they have told us. Sometimes they know that they have told us, and other times they don't know what they have revealed. But Jesus said, "Out of the abundance of the heart, the mouth speaks." If you have been around some-one who has routinely verbalized his envy, or competitive-ness, or anger, or inadequacy, and he has linked them to his troubled marriage, or business partnership, or troubles at the office, then it would be pastoral folly to ignore it.

But here is the key when it comes to adjudicating disputes. Motives don't really matter except to the ex-tent that (in a criminal case) the establishment of mo-tives might pertain to an issue like premeditation. "The defendant told me three months before the murder that he was going to avenge an unconscionable slur upon his character by the deceased. He said the deceased had called him a baby-nut. Twice." But in other ways, our touchy-feely era is way too interested in motives. This is why we now have stiffer penalties for hate crimes (which must be distinguished from those ordinary, run-of-the-mill love crimes). What matters is what was said or done, period. Say we are dealing with a case of slander. It ought not to matter to us if the slander was done for this evil motive or that one. If it was, in fact, slander, which can be established, then whatever the motive was, it had to have been a bad one. But which bad motive it was ought to be left to the pastors and counselors. It is not relevant to the question of administering justice.

If the pastor did pilfer from the offering, his motives may be pastorally relevant, but they are not relevant to whether he should be deposed from office. And if he was falsely accused of doing this by a deacon, the fact that the deacon did it out of envy is pastorally relevant, but it is not relevant to whether he should be removed from the diaconate for his slander. Rightly balanced and rightly known, motives matter to persons, and in personal relationships, but there are important places in our consideration where we do not and must not factor them in.

BLOODLESS SYLLOGISMS

Jesus taught us to evaluate arguments and doctrines on the basis of the lifestyle of the teachers—by their fruits ye shall know them. But gnostics want detached, abstracted arguments that can be evaluated in the pristine laboratory of the brain. Gnostics like to pretend that the *ad hominem* is necessarily out of bounds, always and forever, which means, of course, that while their argument is not "to the man," it is rather against the Son of man, which is worse.

We should all understand the variations on this theme. The sun will rise in the east tomorrow even if a jerk today maintains loudly that it will. And someone who appears to be a very nice man can propagate damnable heresies. Because Satan's emissaries will frequently appear as ministers of righteousness, there are more than a few situations that require a second look. So there is a sense in which the *ad hominem* can be a fallacy, and there are times when it takes more than ten minutes for the bad fruit to become manifest.

But the central fact remains: Jesus taught us that ungodliness, malice, hatred, bitterness, pride, envy, and backbiting are all forms of behavior which, when displayed, refute the carrier. The man who shrilly demands that others "deal with his arguments" instead of dealing with his obvious race-baiting or self-importance or whatever else is a man who is trying to replace the fruit of the Spirit with bloodless (and therefore dead) syllogisms.

Leaving room for the judgment of God is part of true justice. People with sinful motives are not unseen; they are (like the rest of us) naked before God; and He is not mocked. It is true that all people reap what they sow (the Bible tells me so); in due time their foot will slide. In fact, bitterness, envy, hatred, and the like are judgments in themselves. They are corrosives that eat their own containers. Stand back. "The Lord is known by the judgment He executes; the wicked is snared in the work of his own hands" (Ps. 9:16).

CHAPTER 9

TRIAL *by* INTERNET

These six things the LORD hates,
Yes, seven are an abomination to Him:
A proud look,
A lying tongue,
Hands that shed innocent blood,
A heart that devises wicked plans,
Feet that are swift in running to evil,
A false witness who speaks lies,
And one who sows discord among brethren.

PROVERBS 6:16-19

Most people believe that technology is a staunch friend.
There are two reasons for this. First, technology is a friend.
It makes life easier, cleaner, and longer. Can anyone ask
more of a friend? Second, because of its lengthy, intimate,
and inevitable relationship with culture, technology does not
invite a close examination of its own consequences. It is the
kind of friend that asks for trust and obedience, which most
people are inclined to give because its gifts are truly bountiful.
But, of course, there is a dark side to this friend. Its gifts are
not without a heavy cost. Stated in the most dramatic terms,
the accusation can be made that the uncontrolled growth of
technology destroys the vital sources of our humanity. It creates
a culture without a moral foundation. It undermines certain
mental processes and social relations that make human life
worth living. Technology, in sum, is both friend and enemy.

NEIL POSTMAN

T he Bible tells us that the man who is able to tame the tongue is able to deal with anything. The tongue is a restless evil, James says, full of poison. It sets the world on fire, and is set on fire by hell. As long as sin has been in the world, this has been true, but whenever new means of communication are developed, sin eagerly rushes in, often before cultural sanctification and manners catch up with it.

NEW APPLICATIONS OF GOD'S WORD

As a new technology, the internet has presented some fresh challenges to the world, and especially to the church. Technology enables men to do many things faster, bigger, and with less effort. In and of themselves, technologies are neither good nor evil. On the other hand, the men who make use of them *are* good or evil (or both). Explosives can move mountains or wipe out cities. The printing press was invented and was gloriously used by God to spread the availability of the Scriptures. But the same printing press made scurrilous broadsheets and pamphlets possible, and those applications were not slow in coming. The telephone was invented and made many wonderful things possible, but gossip and time-wasting chatter were right there as well.

Now we are dealing with the internet, email, and the like, and all the warnings that St. James gave us must be taken to heart in new ways. We are dealing with the electronic tongue, and we have not yet learned how to handle the electronic tongue. To the extent that pastors talk about the internet in sermons at all, it tends toward concerns about pornography. This is far from being an unreasonable concern, because porn is a big problem, but I think Scripture also encourages us to address the sins that are commonly and routinely committed by people in front of other Christians. Christians who use porn almost always sneak off to do it alone, in secret. But disgraceful websites are set up for the whole world to see, and the problem is not recognized for what it is. We are so much in the grip of radical individualism that as long as someone is advancing something that he calls his perspective or point of view, we think in First Amendment terms rather than in Second Greatest Commandment terms. But points of view are not self-authenticating. They are not autonomous. And to apply Dilbert to this, "When did ignorance become a point of view?"

With this in mind, let us just note a few sins of the electronic tongue. They are all particular applications of principles found in Scripture, revealed to us long before the day of ones and zeros. But we have to remember that we are creatures of habit in our virtues and vices, and this means that people will often do in a new setting something they would never dream of doing in an older, more familiar setting. This is because the older, more familiar setting was governed by a set of manners that were seeking (sometimes rightly, sometimes wrongly) to govern that behavior. But when the setting changes, all bets are off. In a previous era, pietistic churches often had rules against going to the movies in a theater, which used to be the only place you could see films. But with the advent of television, the DVR, DVDs, and streaming video, members of such churches can watch movies without a twinge in their conscience. Men who would never dream of buying a pornographic magazine will visit pornographic websites. And bringing us to the point, people will type things at a keyboard that they would never dream of *saying*.

NO NEUTRALITY

While technology might be neutral, men are not. Now, instead of a gossip being able to ruin a reputation in a local community alone, the World Wide Web can now spread malice to the globe. This gives a man a megaphone with which he can sin. All you need is a keyboard and a service provider. One recent hack proudly announced that he had reached three thousand new people in one month. So, is this a good thing? Does the multiplication of sin make this a better world? And we must remember, for gossip and slander to do their murderous work, there must also be recipients. It takes at least two for gossip to do its dirty deed. We now have millions who feed regularly on this degrading roughage. There are many who eavesdrop (or lurk) in the blogosphere and run with what they read. It is important to remember that what you have read (or heard) is not the same thing as what you know.

Here are just a few things to watch for:

1. *Trial by Internet.* The principles of justice are to be applied by individual Christians who are faithful members of churches, sessions of elders, faithful presbyteries, and councils of Christians. They are all to be dealt with in an incarnational way, settled and applied by people who live with one another, and love one another in three-dimensional ways. When someone's reputation is being dragged through the mud, we have to remember to give an attack website the same authority (i.e., none) that we would give a Xeroxed nasty-gram tacked to a telephone pole. Scurrilous sites are easy to identify, and Scripture requires us *to ignore them completely.* Not only should we ignore them completely, we should ignore those who do not distance themselves from everyone engaged in that kind of thing.

   Other sites are not scurrilous, and make a great show of putting on a dignified air, but they are still attempting to try the case in the wrong place. Jesus did not say, "And if your brother does not hear you, I hear blogs are fairly inexpensive."

2. *Speed Is Not Synonymous With Truth.* We used to equate a fast talker with a greater likelihood of falsehood. This suspicion ought to remain with us. What the internet does is enable us to circulate our ignorance around the globe at high speed. The

fact that I can click a button, and a few seconds later people in Australia can read what I wrote does not make it right. Jesus said of the Pharisees that they made a great business of crossing over land and sea to make a convert, and when they made one, he became twice as much a son of hell as themselves. You sell what's on the shelves. You export what you produce. You say what's in your heart. If what you have is a pack of lies, or poorly researched slanders, or plain old-fashioned carelessness or folly, then that is what goes up, ever so quickly, when you click the button.

3. *The Internet Is Not Private Space.* Many who sit behind keyboards make the same mistake as a toddler who hides by covering his eyes. If he can't see others, they must not be able to see him. There is truly a weird phenomenon going on here. A few years ago, a couple who both worked at the same establishment posted some homemade pornographic material on the web. Their employer found out about it and dismissed them. They, in turn, sued the employer *for invading their privacy.* Think about that for a minute.

Another illustration of this kind of a strange mind-bend is the phenomenon of what should be called the Narcissistic Blog. A private diary is a private diary, and people can have private pity parties in them. But a narcissistic blog is not private and cannot by any stretch of the imagination be considered private. But on more than one occasion we have seen young people surprised that their elders knew about something. "How did you know that?" "Well, you posted it on the *World Wide Web*." Here's a thought (not quite in jest): larger churches ought to bring an elder on staff whose sole job would be to monitor the blogs of the young people in the church. As Yogi Berra once said, "You can observe a lot by just watching."

4. *Courage is Personal.* When you have something against your brother, or your brother has something against you, buy him a beer and talk to him about it. Commit yourself to it over time. Do everything you can to deal with problems the way a courageous man would, if he were here.

BLOGS AND ACCUSATIONS

There is often a whirlwind of speculative information flying around any community; sometimes it reaches category F5. It is always wise to take shelter from such storms. Their sole purpose is destructive. Tornadoes never build anything. Justice lifts; injustice tears down. "Let no corrupt word proceed out of your mouth, but what is good for necessary edification, that it may impart grace to the hearers" (Eph. 4:29). Many websites exist primarily as dumpsites for recycled accusations. The bitterness of one disgruntled church member with a website can defile way more than the old one-on-one methods.

Experienced Christians are sufficiently aware of these kinds of sins and know what to do with them: ignore them; don't give them the time-of-day; delete; never share. Mature Christians are not about to believe charges of "corruption" and "dishonesty" that are made for no other reason than that the accuser doesn't agree with a couple of books a pastor wrote. Accusations must be proven, and proven in a manner consistent with biblical justice.

SUMMARY EXHORTATION

1. Remember the Golden Rule.

2. Don't demonize motives.

3. Check with the other side before going public.

4. Evaluate your criticisms to see if they are weighty enough to warrant public controversy.

5. Avoid anonymity.

6. Guard against substituting quantity of words for quality of argument.

7. Love accountability.

8. Respect privacy.

9. Don't vent your feelings (Prov. 29:11).

10. Remember that incarnate Christian living matters.

When an accusation, conflict, or controversy arises in a church, denomination, or other entity, and this becomes public, the first thing to remember is that everyone involved needs to honor and respect (and pray for) the principals in the situation, which would include the leaders, the congregation, the accusers, and the accused. These are the entities and persons involved, and they have ways of addressing us all if they want to say something. Responsible Christians everywhere should wait patiently while responsible adults sort out the issues.

A good deal of the inflammatory aspect of many controversies comes from outside—from those who are not directly involved. If you come across a rogue website, remember that the principles of justice are not just academic abstractions. Anyone running such a site should take it down in repentance and tears, and anyone remotely associated with such a site should walk away from it and never look back. Scurrilous attacks do nothing but discredit those who mount them and those who listen to them. Tertullian said, "What a man should not say he should not hear. All licentious speech; every idle word is condemned by God. The things which defile a man in going out of his mouth, defile him also when they go in his ears."[1]

---

1. Tertullian, cited in Philip Schaff, *History of the Christian Church, Volume II: Ante-Nicene Christianity, A.D. 100–325* (Associated Publishers and Authors, 1852–92 reprint) 155.

The comeback may be that some of these attacks from *outside* are being mounted by those who used to be *inside*, and so they have firsthand knowledge. But any responsible individual with firsthand knowledge should be supplying that information to the appropriate bodies involved privately. To the extent that they take the show on the road (and team up with detractors who are discreditable on other grounds), to that same extent they are demonstrating just how unreliable that firsthand knowledge must be. It often turns out to actually be firsthand ignorance.

The second principle is this: Some websites will gather a powerful amount of "information" and lots of links to other attack sites or purported proofs. When you are shoveling excrement, the basic operating strategy has to be one of moving total tonnage. Many of the things claimed are things that most people have no personal knowledge of (except for the way the charges were being made). It is not unusual to find mixed in with all this slanders that others do have personal knowledge of. And guess what? These guys are about as reliable as any other guy with a spittle-flecked keyboard. So honor legitimate authority. Dishonor character-assassination websites. That kind of scurrilous behavior is one reason why prayers of imprecation are in the Bible.

Our point is that those who jump into situations like this with glee and who cut loose with scurrilous attacks are, on the face of it, not to be trusted with *anything*. It is also necessary to refuse to countenance anything from people who are associated with the character assassins but who do not participate in any direct attacks themselves. The unconverted Saul never actually threw any of the stones at Stephen; he just held the cloaks.

It is important to note that some folks cannot tell the difference between the long and honored literary tradition of satire and the equally long and *dishonored* tradition of scurrility. We approve of the former and disapprove of the latter. In this we have the support of all of Western civilization. A second point is related to this: not only can people approve the former and disapprove the latter, as we do, but it should be noticed how some people reverse this. There are many who have no problem with scurrilous attacks but who become positively indignant about biblical satire. Some of the *nastiest* attacks come from people who belonged to the school of thought that would outlaw Erasmus, the prophet Amos, Swift, or Horace. So it is not quite true that these folks cannot tell the difference. They usually can tell the difference between the two approaches—they have just inverted the values (Isa. 5:20).

Everyone should let the governing bodies involved in these kinds of matters sort it all out in a godly and charitable way. But in the meantime, the only course of action that should be obvious to godly Christians everywhere is that of ignoring and despising attack sites that savage men's reputations. These sites despise their responsibility under the ninth commandment to be guardians of their brother's good reputation and name. In this, the pagan officials of

Ephesus have more wisdom than our internet vigilantes. "Wherefore if Demetrius, and the craftsmen which are with him, have a matter against any man, *the law is open*, and there are deputies; *let them implead one another*. But if ye enquire any thing concerning other matters, *it shall be determined in a lawful assembly*" (Acts 19:38–39).

BRAYING CONTESTS

In these days of web slander, what should a ministry's rule of thumb be in responding to such things? There are two basic principles to remember.

First, if a charge has any surface plausibility at all, or any possible traction, do not let it go unanswered. The Scriptures are full of vigorous replies to various saucy coppersmiths. But it is not necessary to spend the rest of your life doing this, answering every detail, because the kind of heart that does this sort of thing is good at spinning out details, frequently *ex nihilo*, and *then* you have hopped on the little hamster cage wheel. But if you answer the central charges forcefully, cogently, and scripturally, then you have given any fair-minded individuals who hear about it all that they need. "Okay, this is clearly a Proverbs 18:17 situation." Sometimes, when this is done well, the result is that strife breaks out between the Sunni and Shia factions of the web insurgency. To change the metaphor, when cannibals run out of missionaries, they sometimes start looking at one another sideways through narrowed eyes. And this is not, incidentally, a sign of disinterested objectivity. A cannibal should not expect to be praised for his impartiality in this.

The second principle is the flip side of this. Don't be so hasty or eager to answer critics that you create opportunities or venues for them that they would not otherwise have. There is a way of answering an opponent that establishes him as an opponent. In other words, don't lend credibility to the incredible. Let them try to make their bricks without straw.

These sorts of questions are fluid and constantly changing. Someone might need to be answered at one point, but three years later, the same person needs to be completely ignored (Prov. 26:4–5). Or vice versa.

So don't answer when it gives irrational critics access to your microphone. Don't refuse to answer when they have some sort of microphone of their own. And when you answer, give an answer that is sufficient for any honest reader, and don't trouble yourself over the dishonest readers. Never get into a braying contest with donkeys.

CHAPTER 10

JUSTICE *and* CHARACTER

But also for this very reason, giving all diligence,
add to your faith virtue, to virtue knowledge, to knowledge
self-control, to self-control perseverance, to perseverance
godliness, to godliness brotherly kindness, and to brotherly
kindness love. For if these things are yours and abound,
you will be neither barren nor unfruitful in the knowledge
of our Lord Jesus Christ. For he who lacks these things is
shortsighted, even to blindness, and has forgotten
that he was cleansed from his old sins.

2 PETER 1:5–9

T he characters of people are proven over time. Therefore, justice can seem slow. All people sin; they sin with their minds, their bodies, and their tongues. But give a person enough time and opportunity, and he will prove what kind of person he really is. People can run, but they cannot hide from themselves, and they certainly cannot hide from God. "Be sure your sin will find you out" (Num. 32:23) and you will reap what you sow (Gal. 6:7).

The stories of the Bible are not given simply to entertain us. All the characters of the Bible are still with us. The stories are given to teach us about God and men, about good and evil, about blessings and curses, about life and death, and about justice and character. Let's consider the historical account of a man named Shimei. It will give us insight as to what we can expect to unfold in the cases of those who think they can throw dust up in the air and unjustly attack others. Their fifteen minutes of fame will not have a happy ending. Shimei didn't have a website or blog, but if he could have, he would have: www.shimei.com.

During the attempted coup against King David by his son Absalom, a Benjamite named Shimei, emboldened by the thought that David's rule had ended, began to publicly insult and attack the king. He clearly saw an opportunity to vent his outrage at David. David was vulnerable, and Shimei thought he was down for good. He was now ready to kick and gouge (from a distance, of course). David remained humble.

> Now when King David came to Bahurim, there was a man from the family of the house of Saul, whose name was Shimei the son of Gera, coming from there. He came out, cursing continuously as he came. And he threw stones at David and at all the servants of King David. And all the people and all the mighty men were on his right hand and on his left. Also Shimei said thus when he cursed: "Come out! Come

> out! You bloodthirsty man, you rogue! The LORD has
> brought upon you all the blood of the house of Saul,
> in whose place you have reigned; and the LORD has
> delivered the kingdom into the hand of Absalom your
> son. So now you are caught in your own evil, because
> you are a bloodthirsty man! (2 Sam. 16: 5–8)

Shimei's bitterness was manifest. He had been loyal to
Saul, and apparently viewed Saul's death as having been
caused by David. Absalom now sat on the throne, and
Shimei seized the moment in order to humiliate David.

Of course his limited knowledge of the matter, cou-
pled with his bitterness, arrogance, and presumption, led
him to false conclusions that he proclaimed loudly and
publicly. In fact, there's a huge difference between what we
know and what we have heard. David had accomplished
more in a week than this man would in a lifetime, but
Shimei could only twist the truth, and he found that every
fact conformed to his perverted view of David.

> Then Abishai the son of Zeruiah said to the king,
> "Why should this dead dog curse my lord the king?
> Please, let me go over and take off his head!" But the
> king said, "What have I to do with you, you sons of
> Zeruiah? So let him curse, because the LORD has said
> to him, 'Curse David.' Who then shall say, 'Why have
> you done so?'" And David said to Abishai and all his
> servants, "See how my son who came from my own
> body seeks my life. How much more now may this

Benjamite? Let him alone, and let him curse; for so the LORD has ordered him. It may be that the LORD will look on my affliction, and that the LORD will repay me with good for his cursing this day." And as David and his men went along the road, Shimei went along the hillside opposite him and cursed as he went, threw stones at him and kicked up dust. Now the king and all the people who were with him became weary; so they refreshed themselves there. (2 Sam. 16:9–14)

David's loyal men saw the injustice being heaped upon their king. They had the power to crush Shimei, and that's what they wanted to do. They considered him to be a "dead dog." It would be difficult to be lower than this. Nevertheless, David understood an important principle: not everything that can be done should be done; not everything that can be said should be said. There is a time and a place for everything. David saw beyond the moment, beyond the injustice, and beyond the aggravation. He saw the providential hand of the Lord. He understood that God was the ultimate dispenser of justice and that in time the blessings and the curses would come.

Absalom (and therefore Shimei) had a reversal of fortune. When Absalom's and David's armies met for battle, the conflict ended with Absalom's death. David reascended to the throne, and thus Shimei's circumstances dramatically changed. He knew it was time for him to sing a different song. Being the brave man of principle that he was, he knew that it was in his best interest to kiss up to David, and so, as David journeyed back to Jerusalem, Shimei used the occasion to apologize to the newly reinstated king. David was incredibly gracious to Shimei, but David was not stupid. He knew what Shimei was up to and that, given the opportunity, Shimei would do whatever he could to facilitate another *coup d'état*. He comprehended the *character* of this man, and he knew that character would eventually manifest itself again. Give people time and opportunity, and they will show the world who they are—give them enough rope and they will hang themselves.

> And Shimei the son of Gera, a Benjamite, who was from Bahurim, hastened and came down with the men of Judah to meet King David. There were a thousand men of Benjamin with him, and Ziba the servant of the house of Saul, and his fifteen sons and his twenty servants with him; and they went over the Jordan before the king. Then a ferryboat went across to carry over the king's household, and to do what he thought good. Now Shimei the son of Gera fell down before the king when he had crossed the Jordan. Then he said to the king, "Do not let my lord impute iniquity to me, or remember what wrong your servant did on the day that my lord the king left Jerusalem, that the king should take it to heart. For I, your servant, know that I have sinned. Therefore here I am, the first to come today of all the house of Joseph to

go down to meet my lord the king." But Abishai the son of Zeruiah answered and said, "Shall not Shimei be put to death for this, because he cursed the LORD's anointed?" And David said, "What have I to do with you, you sons of Zeruiah, that you should be adversaries to me today? Shall any man be put to death today in Israel? For do I not know that today I am king over Israel?" Therefore the king said to Shimei, "You shall not die." And the king swore to him. (2 Sam. 19:16–23)

David was grateful and happy to have been restored, and he sought no revenge. His men were still ready to swiftly remedy the problem of Shimei with a sword, yet David held them back once again. He wasn't going to let the likes of Shimei ruin the joy of his celebration. Bitter men are not content to destroy themselves; they always seek to defile others. Moreover, David was wise—he was above this and refused to allow this man to rob him of what God had given him. Again, David was no fool. He was not deceived by the kind of man Shimei was; but David was a bigger man. Grace is a powerful force.

Along the way, many of David's loyal men continued to want to see Shimei taken out, yet David refused to follow that counsel. As he neared the end of his life, this wise father met with his son and successor, Solomon, to give some parting counsel. He warned him about Shimei, who would continue to be a threat to Israel's king:

> And see, you have with you Shimei the son of Gera, a Benjamite from Bahurim, who cursed me with a malicious curse in the day when I went to Mahanaim. But he came down to meet me at the Jordan, and I swore to him by the Lord, saying, "I will not put you to death with the sword." Now therefore, do not hold him guiltless, for you are a wise man and know what you ought to do to him; but bring his gray hair down to the grave with blood. (1 Kings 2:8–9)

Now as we know, Solomon was no fool. This wise man kept a close eye on this contentious and duplicitous man. He knew the words of Moses: "Vengeance is Mine, and recompense; their foot shall slip in due time; for the day of their calamity is at hand, and the things to come hasten upon them" (Deut. 32:35). Solomon was willing to wait for the corrupt character of Shimei to bubble up again. When the time was right, Shimei would stumble into a trap of his own making and Solomon would deal with him accordingly by placing him under house arrest and confining him to Jerusalem.

> Then the king sent and called for Shimei, and said to him, "Build yourself a house in Jerusalem and dwell there, and do not go out from there anywhere. For it shall be, on the day you go out and cross the Brook Kidron, know for certain you shall surely die; your blood shall be on your own head." And Shimei said to the king, "The saying is good. As my lord the king

has said, so your servant will do." So Shimei dwelt in
Jerusalem many days. (1 Kings 2:36–38)

Solomon isolated the bigmouth to limit his influence.
As long as Shimei kept his word and stayed confined to
his narrow circle, Solomon left him alone. Yet Solomon
knew this arrogant man—he could neither keep his word
nor close his mouth. Shimei broke the agreement and was
executed by Solomon. God takes our words very seriously.

> Now it happened at the end of three years that
> two slaves of Shimei ran away to Achish the son of
> Maachah king of Gath. And they told Shimei, saying,
> "Look, your slaves are in Gath." So Shimei arose, sad-
> dled his donkey, and went to Achish at Gath to seek
> his slaves. And Shimei went and brought his slaves
> from Gath. And Solomon was told that Shimei had
> gone from Jerusalem to Gath and had come back.
> Then the king sent and called for Shimei, and said
> to him, "Did I not make you swear by the LORD, and
> warn you, saying, 'Know for certain that on the day you
> go out and travel anywhere, you shall surely die?' And
> you said to me, 'The word I have heard is good.' Why
> then have you not kept the oath of the LORD and the
> commandment that I gave you?" The king said more-
> over to Shimei, "You know, as your heart acknowledg-
> es, all the wickedness that you did to my father David;
> therefore the LORD will return your wickedness on
> your own head. But King Solomon shall be blessed,

and the throne of David shall be established before the LORD forever." So the king commanded Benaiah the son of Jehoiada; and he went out and struck him down, and he died. Thus the kingdom was established in the hand of Solomon. (1 Kings 2:39–46)

Now Shimei reluctantly stayed in bounds for about three years, but in due time he grew careless. Two of his servants had all they could take of Shimei, so they took off for Gath, and he decided to go after them. Solomon received word of his departure from Jerusalem and called for his arrest. Now he stood before King Solomon and it was time for this evil man to face the music. Having made a promise to his father, Solomon now executed that promise by having Shimei executed. Shimei's words had finally borne their bitter fruit. The bad guys always lose. Solomon would later write:

Then I saw the wicked buried, who had come and gone from the place of holiness, and they were forgotten in the city where they had so done. This also is vanity. Because the sentence against an evil work is not executed speedily, therefore the heart of the sons of men is fully set in them to do evil. Though a sinner does evil a hundred times, and his days are prolonged, yet I surely know that it will be well with those who fear God, who fear before Him. But it will not be well with the wicked; nor will he prolong his days, which are as a shadow, because he does not fear before God. (Eccles. 8:10–13)

"The tongue of the wise uses knowledge rightly, but the mouth of fools pours forth foolishness. The eyes of the LORD are in every place, keeping watch on the evil and the good. A wholesome tongue is a tree of life, but perverseness in it breaks the spirit" (Prov. 15:2–4). Perhaps this was a proverb that came from Solomon's experience with Shimei. Man's ways are predictable. The wages of sin are still death. He is the Lord of time, space, and even cyberspace.

CHAPTER 11

ANONYMITY

And this is the condemnation, that the light has come into the world, and men loved darkness rather than light, because their deeds were evil. For everyone practicing evil hates the light and does not come to the light, lest his deeds should be exposed. But he who does the truth comes to the light, that his deeds may be clearly seen, that they have been done in God.

JOHN 3:19–21

Never write what you dare not sign. An anonymous letter-writer is a sort of assassin, who wears a mask, and stabs in the dark. Such a man is a fiend with a pen. If discovered, the wretch will be steeped in the blackest infamy.

CHARLES SPURGEON

A s we have explained throughout this book, anonymity is always a favorite perch from which to fire accusations. "Don't tell anyone I told you this, but . . ." Add to this the amplifier of the internet, and the snipers have found a new long-range weapon. From a distance, shots can be fired; cowards can hide. Even when real names are used (and they often are not), there are many who will vent their spleens in cyberspace who would never have the courage (or foolishness) to do so to another man's face.

Tim Challies wrote that "Admiral Lord Nelson once remarked that 'every sailor is a bachelor when beyond Gibraltar.' This was a statement about anonymity, something that was quite rare just a few generations ago. Nelson knew that once his sailors moved beyond the bounds of the British Empire, beyond society's systems of morality and accountability, they underwent a transformation. Every man became 'single' and sought only and always his own pleasure. Os Guinness remarks that in the past 'those who did right and those who did not do wrong often acted as they did because they knew they were seen by others. Their morality was accountability through visibility.'"[1]

Now since technology constantly changes, we must evaluate what lies behind its abuses and apply biblical principles to these new circumstances.

NAMELESS OTHERS

Chesterton famously spoke of tradition as the democracy of the dead. He thought we ought not exclude someone's voice from a discussion on the technical grounds that they were not still alive. The point is well-taken, but there are

1. Tim Challies, "Behind Closed Doors," (http://www.challies.com /articles/behind-closed-doors). Os Guinness, *The Call* (Nashville: Thomas Nelson, 1998), 88. Cited by Tim Challies.

some discussions and arguments where voices ought to be excluded. We are not referring to the voices of the disembodied dead, but rather to the voices of the disembodied complainers and accusers. We are referring to the "nameless others."

When someone brings a concern to people in authority, whether in a school, church, village, or whatever, it is frequently found that he is representing quite a number of "nameless others." "Quite a few people feel exactly the way I do about this." "Really? Who feels this way?" "Well . . . I promised not to say."

This kind of thing is bad enough in group discussions and decision-making, as in a school. "I don't think the school board should build the new annex, and everybody I know feels the same way." It's an attempt to hold elections on the sly, have just your friends vote, and then announce the results to those who have the temerity to disagree with you. This sort of thing appeals to a certain kind of mind but is repulsive to those who want to administer and govern justly. Those for whom nameless others have any kind of authority at all are people who have not understood the most basic biblical principles of justice.

It gets worse though. Not only do nameless others want to do the opposite of "stand up and be counted" (they want to hide themselves away and be counted) in situations like "building an annex," they also frequently use the device to make accusations. The accusations, however, are not against nameless others, but rather against specially named others. The wicked bend the bow and put the arrow on the string. And why? So that they might shoot *secretly* at the upright in heart (Ps. 11:2).

Suppose that an anonymous accuser has publicly charged me with lying (just suppose, all right?). There is an entire series of instructive opportunities that fall out from this.

First, someone might say that I just want to know the name of the person so that I can conduct an *ad hominem* attack on him. So let's talk about that. An *ad hominem* attack is an informal fallacy, a fallacy of distraction. That is, it is an informal fallacy when it is a fallacy, which arguing "to the man" often isn't. Arguing "to the man" is only a problem when the man is not the point. If a man is saying that salt is white, and I disregard his statement because he is a jerk who mistreats his mother, I am guilty of the *ad hom* fallacy. But if his mother was murdered, and he is on trial for that murder, his relationship to his mother is not an extraneous issue being brought in to discredit him. It is the central issue. Under those circumstances, to exclude evaluation of character and insist that we simply "weigh the disembodied arguments" is to be guilty of another fallacy of distraction. When we all stand before the throne of God, He is going to evaluating *persons*, not arguments. And the only salvation for people like us will be to be found in the *Person* of Jesus Christ.

To act as though arguments have any kind of substance apart from the lives of those advancing them (when it comes to accusations) is to be guilty of the worst forms of Enlightenment rationalism. And because Enlightenment rationalism still has a significant purchase in many hearts and minds, it can still *sound* objective and dispassionate to say, "Yes, I know that anonymous accusers have said on my website that Jones is wicked, and that he robs banks in his spare time, but they have advanced arguments in favor of this thesis. Rather than obsessing about the anonymous character of the accusation (a technicality, surely?) ought not Jones just answer the arguments themselves?"

No, it is *not* a technicality, and no, the answers to accusations ought never be answered in that kind of a setting. If someone accused me (anonymously) of some nefarious crime, and it was the kind of thing I could disprove in ten seconds, I would still not do it in such a setting. And why? Because when principles of justice are ignored to such an extent, nothing is easier than to pretend that I *only tried to disprove it* but was tragically unsuccessful. These anonymous zealots for truth—they want the truth about everything to be known, except for the truth of their motives and their given names—don't care at all about the truth. If they did, they wouldn't be accusing the way they are from their private place. So why should I submit any argument at all to those who have manifested their contempt for due process? I have better things to do with my time than to seek out unjust judges.

Second, the process is absurd. As we pointed out earlier, anonymous accusations can be received in any direction, and they can then cancel each other out. I do not have to answer my anonymous accusers because (fortunately!) I just received a series of anonymous emails this morning warning me that all my anonymous accusers are making the accusations because they are in the pay of a man who is my mortal enemy. And he is my mortal enemy because I told him to stop cheating on his wife. The entire operation is being run from a minimum security prison, where the ringleader is now residing. He is there, actually, because of his treatment of his previous pastor. When it is objected that I ought not to do this, I reply (trying not to look smug) that I really think we ought to consider the arguments that are being advanced and try our best to keep personalities out of it.

But of course, only Hellenists want to keep personalities out of it. Arguments by themselves are airy-fairy. People sin or are righteous. People lie or tell the truth. People have motives, good or bad. People live successfully in community or they don't. People advance arguments, and they do it well or they do not. People know how to get along. Or they don't.

A.K.A.

A moving target is another form of anonymity; "catch me if you can." Shine the light on those scoundrels in the darkness, and they will scurry back to their holes only to emerge again in a cheap disguise. The disguises are not nearly as good as they think they are. Back when ladies wore slips under their dresses, occasionally their slips would show, and the same is true for those who have dressed up in a pseudonym.

Anonymous letters, emails, and blog comments are often too clever by half. Their character and their vocabulary are revealing. Not that identifying the voice of their actual author can be done infallibly, but it can be done with a high degree of accuracy. They will write under their wife's name or under a series of aliases. After a short time, their voice exposes them, and the boorish pattern repeats itself. And, of course, because our reading of someone's voice can be accurate without being infallible, it is quite possible that once they are unmasked, they will pop up again, this time with a waxed handlebar mustache, claiming again that some grave injustice was done to them. So, it is always appropriate to ask them to identify themselves and give the name of their pastor or some credible references.

The problem is complicated by other bad actors, slandermeisters, coming on with their false identities to carry on their campaign against their most recent target. In a normal situation, there should be no problem with Bob or Jon or Sally carrying on a discussion about theology or politics in an internet space like a blog without providing their last names or other identifiers. But solo names are open to abuse by gunslingers—the sort of people who are, in internet parlance, trolls. They specialize in getting themselves someplace where they can be the center of attention, if only for a brief moment. Trolls always want to make a name for themselves. And whenever they do this under a false solo name, they bring all the other solo names under suspicion, if only for a moment. Whenever a new person piles in, with deep concerns about the matter, let us say, it could be legit, or it could be one more alias chiming in and warming up.

And this is the buildup to the point we want to make about justice. A blog is owned and operated by an individual. It is not a place like Hyde Park, where anybody can just say their piece. It is more like a person's living room, where people are invited to come over, and to talk. It is a private event where the public is invited to participate within certain specified guidelines. Whenever someone signs up to post, that someone is *agreeing* to abide by the rules or guidelines. There are consequences to breaking the rules. If this were a seminar in a rented room at a university, and a questioner was evicted by security for disorderly conduct, and ten minutes later showed up in a false nose and mustache, saying, "No, no, I'm not that other guy . . . but let me continue to try to make his point. I have some primary documents here . . . ," it would not be long before everyone in the audience would see that they were being imposed upon in an egregious way.

A baptized church member has every right to come to the Table, and should not be prevented unless there has been a trial that shows he is violating his baptismal obligations. A citizen of a free nation should have the full presumption of innocence, and his liberty should not be taken away unless his commission of a crime has been proven beyond a reasonable doubt. But an invitation to visit with others in someone's living room is not in the same category. If someone puts their muddy boots on the coffee table repeatedly, despite being asked not to, it is not an injustice to uninvite them. Enrollment in a school, for another example, is a privilege, not a right, and a student can simply be dropped for poor academic performance. This is not an injustice either. Access to certain things is a right. Access to others is a privilege. And access to my living room in order to call me a skunk and a tyrant would be in the latter category, not the former.

Anonymous and alias accusers hide or lie about their identity in order to get into a place where they are un-invited. It is their bad behavior that is the problem, not their name. If they want to participate they don't need to change their name, just their behavior. But changing names is easy with free Google or Yahoo email addresses, and repentance for this kind of problem is very hard. A person who will hide or lie about their own name will have no trouble lying about others.

CHAPTER 12

LYING, WARFARE, *and* PEACE

Therefore, putting away lying, "Let each one of you speak truth with his neighbor," for we are members of one another.

EPHESIANS 4:25

I f living in community offers many options both for building up and for tearing down with a just or unjust tongue. Here are some ways we have identified to "put away lying" and "speak truth with your neighbors."

WEASEL WORDS

Vows, contracts, promises, and other informal commitments are the main ways we enter into and maintain relationships. Psalm 15 describes the character of the man who may dwell with the Lord, and one of those key character traits is described in verse 4: "He who swears to his own hurt and does not change." In the book of James we have a similar admonition: "But let your 'Yes' be 'Yes,' and your 'No,' 'No,' lest you fall into judgment." In other words, a person's character is only as good as his word.

Just as God's words and God's actions are perfectly consistent with one another, He expects the same from us. When we make formal or informal commitments, explicit or implied, we either keep or break them (even when it is difficult). This reveals a great deal about *who* we are. When the heat is on, when it's time to write the check or deliver the goods, we're sometimes tempted to conveniently forget or to try and squirm out. We try a little "revisionist" history. "That's not exactly what was said." Or, "I don't remember us talking about that." "Oh, you took it that way?" Many politicians seem to be professional weasels who know how to use these kinds of spin or weasel words as a constant cover. Justice is dependent on truth— the whole truth.

Weasel words are perfectly good terms used in perfectly empty ways. They are slippery, both in how they are used (to allow the meaning to slide between this or that) and why they are used (to grease the escape route from some unwanted responsibility). Merriam-Webster sheds light on the etymology: "Some people believe that weasels can suck the insides out of an egg without damaging the shell. An egg thus weasel-treated would look fine on the outside, but it would actually be empty and useless. We don't know if weasels can really do that, but the belief that they could caused people to start using 'weasel word' to refer to any term intended to give the impression that everything is fine when the speaker is really trying to avoid answering a question, telling the truth, or taking the blame for something."[1]

A person says what he needs to in order to get what he wants at the moment. "It depends on what the definition of 'is' is." Like the restaurant that had a sign that read "All You Can Eat for $10." Sounding like a great deal, the fellow ordered the plate. When he asked the waitress for a second plate she informed him that it would be an additional $10. The customer pointed to the sign and said "I thought it was all you could eat for $10?" The waitress replied, "Well, sir, that is *all you can eat* for $10."

DECEPTION

Deception is an act of war, and the same distinctions that we make between *murder* and *killing* must be made between *lying* and *lawful deception*. The sinful forms of deception are those which introduce a state of civil war and animosity into communities that ought to be at peace. The ninth commandment is primarily about perjury (although other forms of deception outside of court are certainly subsumed under it). When someone bears false witness against his *neighbor*, he is introducing a state of settled animosity where there ought to be peace. Paul tells the Colossians that they are not to lie *to one another*, seeing how they have put off the old man with its evil practices.

1. "Weasel word," Merriam-Webster, accessed August 2, 2018, https://www.merriam-webster.com/dictionary/weasel%20word.

And this is why the lake of fire is reserved for liars. God hates those who sow discord among the brethren.

But in the course of a just war, deception is not a problem at all. When the Israelites pretended to retreat in the second battle of Ai, this was not a violation of the ninth commandment. When Moses told Pharaoh that he wanted him to let the people go, the request was to let them go for a three-day festival. Neither was this a violation of the ninth commandment. When David pretended to be mad in a foreign court, he was deceiving the king but not breaking the ninth commandment. (In addition to that, his action brought us one of the great comebacks in the Bible. "What's this guy doing here? Did you think I needed more madmen in my entourage? Did you think I had a *shortage*?") Rahab went over to the Israelites, and the Israelites were at war with Jericho. Her deception concerning the spies was not a violation of the ninth commandment, and, as James teaches us, it was the point of her justification. And when the Hebrew midwives misled Pharaoh on why they were not committing infanticide, neither were they breaking the ninth commandment. In fact, God expressly blessed them for what they did.

So assume a just war, lawfully conducted. Is it a lie for a tank commander to drive around in a camouflaged tank, telling the enemy pilots he is a bush when in fact he is not a bush? Is it a sin for an undercover operative crossing a border to say nothing when the security guards look at his false passport? Should he say, "Thanks for the questions, guys. I have been looking for an opportunity to come clean"? Or how about your "Beware of Dog" sign when you don't have a dog, or the fact that you leave a light on in the house when you depart so that potential burglars will think someone is at home? Of course not.

But within the realm where God's law commands and requires peace from us, of necessity, there must be strict truth-telling.

Now Jesus told parables, and He is truth incarnate. This shows us that truth has to be more than a matter of simple correspondence to the world outside. Note that it must be *more* than simple correspondence—not *less*. But for those who have a hermeneutic made out of rough-cut fir, this kind of "subtlety" just exasperates them. And were we lying when we intimated that some people actually have a hermeneutic that is made out of wood? No, because the Bible teaches us that one of the best ways to communicate *truth* is by means of caricature and gross overstatement (camels and needles, blind leading blind, beam and mote, etc.). The fact that some people are so literal-minded that they do not get the jokes (including the jokes of Scripture) does not make those who use such expressions liars. If there is no intent to deceive, there is no lie.

One time, years ago, we put in the masthead of *Credenda/Agenda* a statement to the effect that all the articles had been screened for heresy by some cool software that we had. When we got a letter asking about the software, no one was more astonished than we were. But the problem here is not the use of jokes, figures of speech, parables, and so forth. The Scriptures point us in this direction. In the beginning was the Word, not the Pristine Formula. Banishing all fiction, poetry, metaphors, etc. as essential carriers of ultimate truth is how modernity went so grievously astray. And so the Word brings with Him all that lawful words do. Truth is far more textured than modernists think.

The irony here is that we do not have to teach anyone how to make these distinctions. We make them ourselves, naturally and readily, provided we are the ones accused of being a liar. We were probably able to make all the distinctions about knowledge and intent at the age of two. Our willfulness, our stubbornness, and all the real problems, come when we (for *political* reasons) refuse to extend the charity of these same distinctions to others, including our adversaries.

Because lying is fundamentally an act of war, God hates it. And, flipping it around, this is why unfounded accusations of lying are so destructive. Such assertions set people at odds, they introduce conflict, they stir up mayhem in the world of relationships.

Now stick with this one minute more, because here is the tricky bit. Suppose a number of people have been industriously trying to build up a cottage industry of accusing me of various kinds of nefarious business, and included in my alleged skullduggery is lying. Now, when these people accuse *me* of lying, are *they* lying? Applying the standards we have outlined above, I can't say so. They *might* be, but I can't prove it, so I shouldn't say it. As discussed earlier, someone is a liar when they know that I have spoken the truth, and they say, contrary to this, that I have lied, and they do this in order to get other people to believe it. And if all these conditions pertain (making such a person a liar), and I cannot prove that they pertain, then I still should not make the accusation. In other words, when someone accuses me of perjury I can and must say, "This charge is false." But why would someone bring such a false charge? Lying is one possibility, but there are many others. The other motives that might provoke such a false charge against someone are almost never noble, but this is just another way of saying that lying is not the only sin in the world of defamation.

Divisions in the body of Christ may be noted in two stages. The first is when dividers attempt to rally people to their flag, but with little or no success. Such men must be addressed, but not in the same way as divisions in the second category. The second, and more lamentable condition, is when divisions have settled in and the congregation (or community, or denomination) is in fact divided. Such a condition calls for the highest degree of wisdom. Jeremiah Burroughs observes: "It is a great part of the skill of the minister to divide the Word aright; but this skill of his will be put to the test when he comes to divide the Word among a divided people, to give every part its portion."[2]

2. Burroughs, 16–17.

BUSYBODIES

Jane Austen's Henry Tilney said, "Every man is surrounded by a neighborhood of voluntary spies." A "busybody" is someone who pries (sometimes very subtly) into the affairs of others. They want to "know what's going on" in everybody else's life: their marriage, their kids, their finances, etc. They have their finger on the pulse of happenings in the church or the neighborhood, or the school, or the office. It's kind of a "power" position, and even if they don't always use the information they have collected, they nevertheless have it at their disposal in case they need it. Busybodies love to share, usually under the cover of "concern." They are information brokers.

The busybody is constantly making deposits in the account of contention. The irony of the busybody is that they're not busy doing the things they're supposed to be doing. They apparently have too much time on their hands. The house is a mess, the work is undone, the Bible hasn't been read, there's no time for prayer . . . they're too busy with everybody else's business. But there's plenty of time to gather information. There's plenty of time for talk.

Three passages speak to the busybody directly (many speak indirectly).

> For we hear that there are some who walk among you in a disorderly manner, not working at all, but are busybodies. Now those who are such we command and exhort through our Lord Jesus Christ that

they work in quietness and eat their own bread. (2 Thess. 3:11–12)

And besides they learn to be idle, wandering about from house to house, and not only idle but also gossips and busybodies, saying things which they ought not. (1 Tim. 5:13)

If you are reproached for the name of Christ, blessed are you, for the Spirit of glory and of God rests upon you. On their part He is blasphemed, but on your part He is glorified. But let none of you suffer as a murderer, a thief, an evildoer, or as a busybody in other people's matters. Yet if anyone suffers as a Christian, let him not be ashamed, but let him glorify God in this matter. (1 Pet. 4:14–16)

Jesus spoke of judgment for every idle word, and the term He used, referred to unemployed words, lazy words, inactive words, words that don't accomplish much good.

PIOUS SENTIMENT

One of the reasons why pious sentiment is so popular is that it makes a great substitute for obedience. And while we are disobeying what the Bible says to do, the disobedience can be carried off in the glow of self-approbation.

The Bible has some very clear instructions about the handling of charges against someone and on our moral responsibility to steer clear of entertaining unsubstantiated grievances. Let us consider one of the things we do *instead*.

Suppose someone comes to you and says that they are really having trouble respecting and loving their pastor, because last night at two in the morning he crept into their backyard and shot their family dog. What would a biblical response be? And what would a sentimentalist response be?

The pious and sentimental response would urge upon the purveyor of this information the need to be loving, to refrain from bitterness, to return good for evil, to hope for reconciliation, along with mounds and piles of other sweet responses. All the attitudes that are being urged *are* biblical attitudes. So the person urging them is being biblical, right? No. They are among the appropriate responses to such an outrage if the pastor in fact had shot the family dog. But if he did not, and the charge is a false one, then all the pietist has succeeded in doing is covering over some radical disobedience (his and the other guy's) with a couple of gallons of scriptural-language whitewash.

The rather stark example of shooting the family dog makes the point clear. But this applies equally to other scenarios. Did the sin actually occur? If it did not, then all the pious phrases in the world are just smarmy wallpaper in the devil's waiting room. The charge might be entirely false. The charge might be "true," but there are circumstances that have been left out of the account that change the nature of the action entirely. The family dog had gone crazy and was attacking a passerby. The commotion woke up the pastor, and he shot the dog, saving the person's life. The mayor is giving the pastor the key to the city in a special ceremony next month. In this case, all the verses about forgiving, forbearing, staying free of bitterness, are still just as bad.

The "godly response" verses apply under two circumstances. One is if the charge is not disputed. "Yeah, I shot your stupid dog. Why? For being *ugly*. Sure, I'll speak into your tape recorder." In such a case, staying free of resentment and so on is not whitewash on top of disobedience. It is straightforward obedience. The second circumstance is if the charge is denied, but an appropriate adjudicatory body has heard the evidence for the charges and found the pastor guilty anyway. In such a situation, it is appropriate to treat him as convicted of the charge even if he continues to deny it.

Now here is a situation that comes up fairly often and involves a principle of justice that is easily overlooked. Suppose I as an individual know of someone's guilt, but am not in a position to *prove* it. What then? I may know that he is guilty, but if I can't prove it, what should my *judicial stance* toward him be? I may not make a public charge that I cannot substantiate under cross-examination. So suppose I see someone commit an egregious sin with my own two eyes. I go to him privately and confront him, and he says something like, "Yeah, I know that you saw me come out of that motel room with that woman, but I also know that you are the only one who saw me. Ha, ha! And if you come around with your busybody two and three witnesses, I will deny everything. Period. Your word against mine." Now suppose this person is a member of my church, and I am looking forward to serving him the Lord's Supper in two days. Do I offer him the bread and wine? You bet. I have *no business* taking any judicial action against him unless my charges can be *independently verified and established*. If they are true, but cannot be established, then he should have a far greater problem coming to the Supper than I should have with him coming to the Supper. He is the one with the problem, not the rest of the church. Scripture has a much greater problem with innocent people being kept away than with guilty people coming. And the guilty people who are eating and drinking condemnation are not eating and drinking someone else's condemnation. They are doing it to themselves. In this sense, we don't need to fence the Table; the Table fences us.

So then, Scripture *requires proof*, and does not allow us to substitute a sanctimonious dodge instead. If I have a charge, then I should prove it, and I should offer my proof to be examined by counter proofs. I may not be allowed to sub in an offer to pray for the person, or to forgive him, or love him in spite of all his Wicked But Heretofore Unproven Crimes.

Someone might dispute all this as a mass of tangled presbyterian legalisms. "Witnesses! Proofs! Cross-examinations! Bah!" But why do they dispute it? Anyone who disputes this is only doing so to cover up their illicit double life as a cruiser of gay bars, not to mention all their shop-lifting at Target. And we think we should pray for him to be delivered from this destructive lifestyle. "But how can you *say* that? You don't even know who will object yet! How can you prove this?" *Prove* it? We still have to do that? Isn't proof a tangled form of presbyterian legalism?

This is just another application of the universal desire that each person has for due process when he is the one being processed. But as for that other guy . . . he doesn't deserve due process. Isn't he the creep who shoots dogs?

BELIEVING A LIE

In our earlier discussions of charges, perjury, etc. we showed that it is contrary to Scripture to allow slander-ers and defamers a free hand. A judiciary proceeding that does not require independent confirmation, does not re-quire cross-examination, and does not hold false witnesses accountable is a judiciary proceeding that has made itself, in principle, an instrument of injustice. It is the judiciary from hell.

This kind of carelessness is culpable. In other words, under these circumstances, it is a *sin* to be lied to: "An evildoer gives heed to false lips; a liar listens eagerly to a spiteful tongue" (Prov. 17:4). As with all proverbs, we have to remember that they do not communicate truth in an "all triangles have three sides" kind of way. Sometimes a bird in the hand is not worth two in the bush. This is the case with scriptural proverbs also. Sometimes lazy people win the lottery, and poverty does not come upon them like a bandit. The truth of that proverb remains, all the same. So, some people who believe a lie are victims. But this proverb tells us that there are some who are lied to who are not victims at all.

An evildoer *listens* to false lips, and an evil man listens to liars. This means that the contrary option, the one followed by the righteous man, is to reject the liar, to refuse to give him the time of day. But when a spiteful tongue comes around a liar, he is operating in a seller's market. The liar listens *eagerly* to words that are passed on by the spiteful tongue. All in all, the acceptance of anonymous testimony is wicked, to waive the requirement of independent confirmation is disobedient, and to hear only one side of the story is evil. This is because the adjudicatory *inside* is supposed to be a seawall against the tumult of the mob *outside*. When rumors fly through the streets, or around the internet, the story can gather quite a head of steam. And when it gathers this head of steam, it can all come together outside the place where justice is supposed to be administered and loudly demand somebody's head. But in the scriptural world, it is far, far better to let ten guilty men go free than to convict one innocent man, whether or not the mob likes it.

We are presbyterians. We believe in the system of representative government that presbyterianism exhibits. We believe that this form of government (in its essentials) is ancient, going back at least to the time of Moses.

We believe that the government of the synagogue was essentially presbyterian. We believe that government by representative elders was not just local, but also included broader assemblies, like the Sanhedrin. If this is the case, and all presbyterians that we know of believe that it is, then we should take care to remember that it was a General Assembly, a *presbyterian* court, that convicted the Son of God and demanded His execution. Having the right forms on paper is no protection at all. It is not enough to have righteous governmental blueprints; we must also have righteous men—men to love the truth because they love the Truth.

NOTHING BUT PUSHING AND PULLING

The Scripture takes a dim view of those who like to circulate juicy information. "A talebearer revealeth secrets: but he that is of a faithful spirit concealeth the matter" (Prov. 11:13). But we have to do two things here—we have to note the contrast between the talebearer and the man with a faithful spirit, and we also have note how a lying tongue would try to spin this proverb around.

First, in this scenario, the talebearer is active, and the faithful man is active. The first actively reveals, and the second actively conceals. The talebearer takes steps to make sure the word gets out. The faithful man takes steps to make sure that the "matter" stays in. In this proverb, Solomon has a particular kind of situation in mind. He is assuming that the talebearer doesn't care about the secrets or privacy of others and that the faithful man does. But rather than let the Scripture convict him, the talebearer proceeds to demonstrate the second point, which concerns how this can be spun.

Let's consider the logical options first. Taking all of Scripture together, there are four possible ways to go. First, some matters can be revealed that should not be revealed (Prov. 11:13). Second, some matters are revealed that should be revealed (1 Cor. 11:18). Third, some matters are concealed that should not be concealed (Acts 5:8–9). And last, some matters are concealed that should be concealed (Prov. 11:13).

Because there is a difference between a talebearer and a whistleblower, we must be wise. Covering in love and covering up in a panic are two very different things—that difference having to do with what is covered, and how it is covered.

When someone is a member of a faction or a party, this wisdom is not exhibited. Different situations arise, and the responses are categorized according to what would help the faction or party. We see this kind of thing in Washington politics all the time from both parties. Say you are opposed to the president. When someone in the CIA leaks something damaging to the president, he is "a courageous whistleblower." If someone leaks something damaging to your side, he is "jeopardizing national security." The party line is the template that people use to determine the difference between righteousness or unrighteousness. This way you don't need to know the facts—all you need to know is what side you are on.

No doubt a person could take a false name, set up a website attacking Douglas Wilson the hatemonger, reviling him for his sundry offenses against the Republic. If he were to do so, he would immediately have a cluster of newfound friends praising the pseudonym for his courage and integrity, not knowing the first thing about him. They would know nothing of his courage and integrity—all they would know is what direction this false name was shooting, and that, in this politicized age, would be more than enough.

This is why the biblical standards for ascertaining what actually happened are so crucial—standards like independent confirmation, checking the other side of the story, mutual accountability for accuser and defendant, ability to discern trivial from weighty matters, etc.—because without them, we have nothing but pushing and pulling. As Buffalo Springfield once memorably put it, "Singing songs and they're carrying signs, mostly saying 'Hooray for our side.'"[3] Those for whom the facts don't matter, and who exult in *any* victory for "their side," no matter how obtained, will soon discover (as Eric Hoffer pointed out in *The True Believer*) that it really doesn't matter what side they are actually on. Those who switch sides are not necessarily apathetic; they are often zealous converts. Men who

3. Stephen Stills, "For What It's Worth (Stop, Hey What's That Sound)," 1966.

were far too eager for polemical battle when they were on our side have been far too eager for battle (in just the same way) when they switch sides.

One last point here: once someone has enlisted in "the fellowship of the grievance" (FOG), all other differences with other members of that fellowship fade into the background. Adversaries become cobelligerents, and then cobelligerents mysteriously become allies. And all because of the shared grievance, which almost assumes a quasi-sacramental status. FOG truly becomes a tie that binds. Vultures of a feather flock together.

CHAPTER 13

VICTIMS *and* JUSTICE

Shall the throne of iniquity, which devises evil by law,
Have fellowship with You?
They gather together against the life of the righteous,
And condemn innocent blood.
But the LORD has been my defense,
And my God the rock of my refuge.
He has brought on them their own iniquity,
And shall cut them off in their own wickedness;
The LORD our God shall cut them off.

PSALM 94:20–23

When Edmund betrayed his sisters and brother in *The Lion, the Witch and the Wardrobe*, he did so because he felt that he was the victim. This is how the world of rationalization, revenge, and treachery works. And this, of course, has a profound effect on perceptions

In his book *The Scapegoat*, Rene Girard refers to the naive persecutor, the persecutor who does not understand that he is not the victim. "Naive persecutors are unaware

of what they are doing. Their conscience is too good to deceive their readers systematically, and they present things
as they see them."[1] At the end of his book, Girard refers tellingly to the place where Jesus taught us that "the
time cometh, that whosoever killeth you will think that he
doeth God service" (John 16:2). Nothing can be clearer
than the biblical teaching that in a fallen world, our understanding of justice is just as fallen. But as the need for
the Golden Rule illustrates, justice is an arch that has col-
lapsed, but it is still standing on my end. In the things that
concern *me*, we all have a robust sense of justice, together
with all the nuances. What we refuse to do is apply that
same standard to our adversary or enemy.

Of course, the Holy Spirit is given to us in order to
restore the image of Christ in us. This means that we are
regenerated by Him and taught by Him to be ashamed
of ourselves when we give way to simplistic finger-point-
ing—as though all the sin were over there. So it is not the
case that there are two categories of people in the world—
the sinners and the righteous. It is more nuanced than
this. We actually have sinners who refuse to see it and
sinners who have been given the gift of seeing it. Those
who have received that gift do not forget what they have
been delivered from.

Those who are in the grip of sin but refuse to acknowledge it perceive themselves as righteous. And the

1. Rene Girard, *The Scapegoat* (Baltimore: Johns Hopkins University
Press, 1989), 8.

reverse is also true. The publican in the Temple who prayed, "God, be merciful to me, a sinner," went home justified. The Pharisee who prayed, "Lord, what a good boy am I," went home unjustified. The sinner was not a sinner, and the saint was a sinner. The one who exalts himself will be humbled, and the one who humbles himself will be exalted.

One of the means God has for doing this is to write His story in such a way as to reveal different purposes for the Author and some of the characters. Jane Austen and Mr. Collins were both responsible for Collins's words and responses. Austen's purpose was to reveal him as a thundering buffoon, and Mr. Collins's purpose was simply to . . . well, who knows what he was thinking. But he was thinking *something*, and it all made sense to him, and off he went. As God writes dialogue, this is a frequent device of His. He writes a story in which clowns think themselves shrewd, and persecutors think themselves victims.

This latter phenomenon is the reason for many gross miscarriages of justice throughout history. What did the high priest do at the condemnation of Jesus? He tore his robes. "How dare you affront us in this way? How dare you speak your blasphemies in such a way as to defile my priestly ears? And look what you did to my robes!" The high priest was in anguish, and there were people alive at that time, looking at that scene, who would have felt sorry for him and not for Jesus. But as Girard implies, time goes by, and all the delusions evaporate (delusions that afflicted

some of the witnesses caught up in that frenzy). But for
that time, a bad man had done bad things to the high
priest and to all the holy things of Israel. The high priest
was in anguish and pain.

What bad things? Well, no need to muster specifics
and arguments—"you all heard what he said! It's in the
public record." When they had previously assembled their
witnesses, attempting to actually prove something, they
were all falling over each other, contradicting each other,
to such an extent that it was even embarrassing to the
kangaroos in robes running that show trial.

Godly Christian churches have to deal with two kinds
of discipline cases. The first has to do with straightforward breaches of the black-letter law of God. Someone
in the congregation is discovered to have been knocking
over convenience stores or cheating on his wife or selling
cocaine. Caught and confronted, he won't repent, his violation of the law of God is established in an open and fair
church trial, and he is disciplined.

But the second kind of situation is when you must deal
with a divisive brother. In this situation, unlike the first,
the sin is not something that comes before the session the
same way problems from the first scenario do. It is actually a dispute for the control of the session. "I'm not the
defendant," the disrupter proclaims. "It may surprise you
all to learn that I ought to be the judge."

It is not uncommon for people to manipulate individuals or systems in order to justify their victim status.

This is attempted by a variety of means, including the use of selected facts, or the deliberate provocation of leaders in the hope of receiving a certain response that, in turn, would enable them to claim unjust treatment. By using this triple-dog-dare, they have to say and do some outrageous things. The point is not that some form of discipline should not be applied, for it should be, but it will not look the same as disciplining an unrepentant adulterer or bank robber. A divisive brother must be handled with love and firmness, and Scripture gives specific instructions on how to do that, but the circumstances vary. For example, a divisive brother that nobody is listening to is not really divisive, and the church can afford to be more patient.

But this brings us to the point of this line of discussion: Folks who have made appalling and unsubstantiated charges share something in common. Invariably, having delivered the charges (in different venues), they assume the role of victim.

It is one thing for a church to occasionally excommunicate a few of her members for objective violations of God's word—things like desertion of a spouse. The people concerned were unrepentant and didn't like what the church did, but they did not play the victim. Others, however, who heap all manner of calumny on the heads of the church leadership, do so while feeling themselves victimized. Many do this after leaving their church (and were therefore not fit subjects for discipline). In such cases, it is usually wise to treat them with extraordinary patience and forbearance and to act with great tact and pastoral care.

Somehow, when the leadership has been wrongfully accused, they are not "victims" in the sense that word is being used. And yet those who accuse them mysteriously and immediately do become victims in this sense. So the lesson should be that when you wrong someone else, there is a profound need to believe that he wronged you. This is an ancient temptation, an ancient failing, as old as dirt.

But God has given us a new commandment, that we love one another; that we learn how to live in community; that we learn how to avoid feeling like a victim because of the wrong things we have done to others.

DISCIPLINE AND PERSECUTION

"Mythology is the very best school in the training of silence. We never hesitate between the Bible and mythology. We are classicists first, romantics second, and primitives when necessary, modernists with a fury, neoprimitives when we are disgusted with modernism, gnostics always, but biblical never."[2]

Girard's book is a fantastic treatment of the decline and fall of the persecutorial vision. He shows how fundamental this vision is to the unbelieving mind, and how the passion of the Christ has brought an end (in principle) to that way of running the world. In the account of the death of Jesus found in the New Testament, we find

2. Girard, 104–105.

that the vision of the persecutors is "abrogated, broken, and revoked."[3]

We have prophetic intimations of this throughout the Old Testament (particularly in Job and in the Psalms), and of course the fulfillment of all these promises in the life, death, and life again of Jesus.

Part of the pattern that persecutors insist upon is the demand that the designated victim "confess his crimes." The cooperating victim is part of the display. From Oedipus to the self-accusers at Stalin's show trials, the choreographed program requires that the victim be cooperative. The virgin must fling herself into the volcano. And this is one of the central "offenses" that persecutors find in the Psalms, and they are not shy about finding fault with the psalmist's imprecations. The psalmist does not cooperate with the staged lie. He insists on his innocence. He says that his former friends have double-crossed him. He points out that his words are being twisted every day by malicious witnesses. He appeals to God for vindication. This is intolerable insolence, and the persecutors gnash their teeth at him. They circle him like wolves.

The persecutorial mind does not just want to kill the designated victim. He wants to be righteous in having done so, and getting the victim to cooperate is an important part of this process. The persecutor does what he does because he himself feels threatened; he feels like a victim who has narrowly averted disaster . . . by getting rid of the

3. Girard, 103.

real troublemaker. A victim at the stake who remains de-
fiant is guilty of outrage—he is continuing to "persecute"
the man in purple robes who ordered him burnt. This kind
of orchestrated frenzy has occurred many times in the history of the world. And they, the powers of old, were intent
on doing it to Jesus. Clearly, manifestly, they were going
to do what had been done countless times before. It was
the ancient way. It is fitting that one man die instead of
the nation, as the high priest put it, speaking far more
accurately than he knew.

And yet, something was still off. Jesus did not accuse
Himself. He did not accept their assessment of Him. He
didn't call down legions of angels to resist them, but He
did not acquiesce either. "No matter," they must have
thought. "We can clean up the account of it later." And
this is precisely what they would have done, but Jesus
messed it all up *by coming back from the dead*. God really
did vindicate Him, declaring Him with power to be the
Son of God by His resurrection from the dead (Rom. 1:4).

After the resurrection, men with fevered brains have
periodically tried to rebuild the same kind of pagan
empires that used to exist before the Incarnation. But
it cannot happen anymore. And in the same way, they
have also tried (from time-to-time) to resuscitate the old
mob-*demos* approach to scapegoating. But that doesn't
work either. The believing world is saved by the gospel,
and the unbelieving world is haunted by it. The story that
hovers over everyone and everything now is the story of

the Victim-King, Christ and Him crucified. This means that the old trick of lying to the crowds, whipping them into a self-righteous froth, cannot work with the same authority anymore. One man with an open Bible can now stand before all tyrants on lawless thrones. One man with an open Bible and free gospel can now stand in front of a lynch mob and face them all down. The death of Jesus has not removed sin and injustice from the world. The tyrants and mobs can and do take lives, and in the century just past, they have taken millions of them. But what the victory of Jesus *has* done is make it impossible for that injustice to successfully pretend to be something else. The old confidence that the persecutors had is gone, and it is gone forever. Christ is Lord, and He is on the throne. And the King of the universe has scars in His hands, feet, and side that He received from the old judicial system.

They can still say and do what they want, but no longer can the persecutors have the same serene confidence that they are doing the will of the divine. "Having your conversation honest among the Gentiles: that, whereas they speak against you as evildoers, they may by your good works, which they shall behold, glorify God in the day of visitation" (1 Pet. 2:12). They can say all manner of outrageous things against us, but when God intervenes to vindicate His people (as He did vindicate His Son and their Lord), they will have to acknowledge that those they attacked were not evildoers at all, but rather righteous. Christians need to learn how to worship, believe, sing, eat, breathe, and live in this confidence and faith, because it is the only appropriate way to entice the persecutors out of their narrow prison.

"Persecutors always believe in the excellence of their cause, but in reality *they hate without a cause.* The absence of cause in the accusation (*ad causam*) is never seen by the persecutors. It is this illusion that must first be addressed if we are to release all the unfortunate from their invisible prison, from the dark underground in which they are stagnating but which they regard as the most magnificent of palaces."[4]

Conservative Christians, Bible-believing Christians, are frequently tempted to walk away from this glorious aspect of the gospel by woodenly applying some aspect or another of biblical law. In the name of theonomy or traditional values or decency, they frequently have fallen into the trap of doing the "right thing" *in the wrong way.* That wrong way has frequently included the temptation to fall into the persecutorial mindset that Jesus did away with in His death.

This is particularly the case with churches that practice church discipline (as the New Testament requires of us). But church discipline is one thing, and persecution is quite another. Church discipline honors and protects the name of Christ. Persecution, or zealously hounding dissenters, disgraces the name of Christ, and in effect denies the gospel. That this is a perennial temptation for

4. Girard, 103.

Christians who take the Scriptures seriously can be seen in all the attempts that we have seen to get us to take this particular bait. But wise church discipline is not just protecting the church from the sins in question, it should also be handled in such a way as to protect the church from the excesses that historically have been connected to the practice of church discipline. The church must not only discipline its members, it must also discipline *itself.*

Church discipline exists, in part, for the protection of the sheep and, therefore, must not be applied without weighing how that protection will play out. Pretended victims will play it to the hilt: "They kicked me out of the church because I dared to disagree with the pastor." For them, everything becomes a stick to whack you with and, thus, it is wisdom not to provide them with more sticks than necessary. Justice protects the innocent (even the innocent bystanders), and it punishes the guilty. God's discipline often involves giving someone over to their own devices; in due time their foot shall slide. There are many kinds of judgment—some of them are swift; others take time.

If someone really wants to be disciplined by the church, what they really need to do is abandon their wife and kids or knock over a few shops. As far as expressing a poor opinion of the pastor goes, not only will the kingdom survive if some folks don't think he walks on water, it will also survive if some are of the decided opinion that he should sink straight to the bottom, the sooner the better, and good riddance.

CHAPTER 14

DUE PROCESS

One witness shall not rise against a man concerning any iniquity or any sin that he commits; by the mouth of two or three witnesses the matter shall be established. If a false witness rises against any man to testify against him of wrongdoing, then both men in the controversy shall stand before the LORD, before the priests and the judges who serve in those days. And the judges shall make careful inquiry, and indeed, if the witness is a false witness, who has testified falsely against his brother, then you shall do to him as he thought to have done to his brother; so you shall put away the evil from among you. And those who remain shall hear and fear, and hereafter they shall not again commit such evil among you. Your eye shall not pity: life shall be for life, eye for eye, tooth for tooth, hand for hand, foot for foot.

DEUTERONOMY 19:15–21

One of the demands of justice is that it must be pursued decently and in order. A rush to judgment is no justice at all. There are urgent situations that demand some instant judgments, but most often there are good reasons for the wheels of justice to turn slowly. It is not only a matter of speed; it must also be cautious and deliberate. Understanding the process and applying the process is a *part of justice itself.* Good fences make good neighbors, and good rules support the cause of justice. Everyone should know the rules ahead of time, and the Bible has given us such directives.

The family, church, and state are obligated to administer justice and to do so decently and in order. These processes are owed to the persons accused, regardless of who they are, presuming they have standing (i.e., they are a family member, church member, citizen of the state, etc.). These processes also protect the accuser and the bodies that will adjudicate the matter, and thus they are necessary for true justice to prevail. Members of these bodies (e.g., family members, church members, citizens, etc.), also have an *obligation to submit* to these God-ordained authorities. To not do so is to be in contempt and is itself an offense.

For example, in taking membership vows in a church, most of us swore an oath saying that we pledged something like this: "To submit ourselves to the discipline of this church and its elders, as the Scriptures require, and as expressed in the church constitution, graciously receiving both instruction and correction as well as submitting to the judicial sanctions of the church." God takes His own Word seriously, and He also takes our word seriously (even if we don't).

While some ignore or hold the due process of legitimate authorities in contempt (e.g., children toward their parents, church members toward the session, citizens against the civil courts, etc.), this does not provide an excuse for these authorities to ignore or bypass biblical due process. It is all the more reason to be careful to "do justice." The unrighteous often ignore the rules, disregard their own oaths, and show contempt for authority. But a righteous man is a man of God's Word and a man of his own word. He serves God first and then his neighbor.

JUSTICE AND MATTHEW 18

In Chapter 7 we introduced the problem of thinking of Matthew 18 as an all-purpose text for witnesses. Here's a little more on Matthew 18 and "due process."

As we mentioned, it is thought that whenever disagreement of a substantial nature arises, it is necessary to work through the problems by going through the steps of Matthew 18—a sort of 1-2-3 checklist approach. Matthew 18 is describing one situation in which the biblical principles apply, but it is not itself the universal method.

> Moreover if thy brother shall trespass against thee, go and tell him his fault between thee and him alone: if he shall hear thee, thou hast gained thy brother. But if he will not hear thee, then take with thee one or two more, that in the mouth of two or three witnesses every word may be established. And if he shall neglect to hear them, tell it unto the church: but if he neglect to hear the church, let him be unto thee as an heathen man and a publican. Verily I say unto you,

Whatsoever ye shall bind on earth shall be bound in heaven: and whatsoever ye shall loose on earth shall be loosed in heaven. Again I say unto you, That if two of you shall agree on earth as touching any thing that they shall ask, it shall be done for them of my Father which is in heaven. For where two or three are gathered together in my name, there am I in the midst of them. (Matt. 18:15–20)

Notice the particulars here. *If your brother sins against you.* The principles of two and three witnesses apply in all situations where the facts are disputed, but the process here is particularly geared to a private dispute. When Peter compromised at Antioch and withdrew from table fellowship with the Gentiles, did Paul have to follow "Matthew 18" before he confronted him publicly? No, the sin was not against Paul, but against the whole church. The sin was not committed in private, but rather in public. The facts in this situation were not disputed, but rather the dispute was over the meaning of the facts.

Let us say that a well-known Christian leader writes a book denying the Trinity. He is published by a well-known Christian publishing house. I write a review of the book, taking him to task. Invariably, someone is going to contact me and ask if I "followed Matthew 18" first. The answer is no. It is possible that this kind of thing will have attempts at private resolution behind the scenes, but since the offense is public, it has to be addressed, at some level, somehow, in public.

Now this means that I need to be sure of my facts. If I accuse him of heterodoxy on the Trinity, and I do so because of my ignorance of certain things taught by the Cappadocian fathers, then in shooting from the hip in this way, I have wronged him. But I have not wronged him because I didn't follow the Matthew 18 process. I have wronged him because I got it wrong—I misinterpreted what he was publicly doing or saying. But if I interpret it correctly, and the offense was against the Church, not me, publicly done, not privately, then a public correction is certainly in order.

Bringing this to a point of application, when people without accountability undertake to make accusations about an incident that happened thirteen years ago that they did not witness, and they do so on the basis of accounts that they did not read carefully, the Matthew 18 process does not apply. Neither does the Paul and Peter scenario from Antioch apply. What applies would be more like the troublemakers following Paul around, telling people that he says *yes, yes*, and *no, no*. Can't trust anything he says. The Church has always had such "catchers-at-words." They must be answered to the extent that their questions raise pastoral problems. But they *do not have to be answered* because their questions deserve answers.

SCURRILOUS IS AS SCURRILOUS DOES

In ancient Israel, one of the purposes of the Mosaic code was to start putting restraints on the still more ancient practice of blood vengeance. It had been that when a man was killed, a relative of the victim would be "deputized" by his tribe or family to go and execute vengeance. Now clearly, this is the kind of system in which the situation could escalate rapidly out of control.

There were two major "reforms" brought in by Moses that addressed this. The first was the instruction to the magistrate to administer *lex talionis*. This is the famous "eye for eye, tooth for tooth" system. Now in that context, the most obvious thing about this strict justice was the fact that it was not "life for eye, life for tooth." Solomon tells us that "because sentence against an evil work is not executed speedily, therefore the heart of the sons of men is fully set in them to do evil" (Eccles. 8:11). The magistrate was instructed to do his work with scrupulous justice, and in a reasonable amount of time. When justice gets mired in a bureaucratic swamp, you begin to see the stirrings of vigilantism. And when vigilantism takes over, you solve the problems of delay, but the end result is gross injustice. The blood avenger takes out the wrong guy, and a tribal war erupts.

Now given the sinful inclination of men toward taking matters into their own hands, it is not surprising that by the time of Jesus, the "eye for eye" business had been transformed in the popular mind (as it remains to this day) as a justification for taking personal vengeance. But Jesus draws us back to the original point, as does Paul in the conclusion of Romans 12 and the beginning of chapter 13. Paul does not say that vengeance is wrong, but rather that it is a prerogative of God's. "Vengeance is *Mine*, saith the Lord."

A second major "reform" introduced by Moses was the idea of the city of refuge. As the Israelites settled into the land, certain cities were designated as the cities of refuge. This meant that if someone killed another man accidentally in a logging accident, the one guilty of manslaughter could flee to the city of refuge. The blood avenger system did not acknowledge the nuanced difference between manslaughter and premeditated murder. The one hunted by the blood avenger could go to one of the cities of refuge, where he would be safe.

But suppose the events were disputed? He said it was an accident, and the blood avenger outside the walls said it was deliberate. "If it had been *accidental*," might say a reasonable blood avenger, "I would not be here." The cities of refuge were not to protect murderers. "But if any man hate his neighbor, and lie in wait for him, and rise up against him, and smite him mortally that he die, and fleeth into one of these cities: Then the elders of his city shall send and fetch him thence, and deliver him into the hands of the avenger of blood, that he many die. (Deut. 19:10–11)

In short, if the man didn't do it, he could stay. If he did do it, then he was turned over. But this is not settled on the basis of hearsay. Two verses later, we learn that "one witness shall not rise up against a man for any iniquity." Before anybody went turning anybody over, the dispute had to be settled beyond a reasonable doubt, with due process.

This sort of thing must be handled by just, calm, deliberate, and honorable men. In short, not the kind of men who specialize in internet vituperation. Whatever happens, whichever honorable men are sorting through the facts of the case, we can be sure that no one slaps his forehead and says, "What are we *thinking*, guys? Going through the tedious facts like this?! We need to find ourselves a couple of scurrilous websites!" On the upside, it would be lots quicker. On the downside, God hates men like that, and teaches us to sing about them in the psalms. "All day long they twist my words . . . ."

CHAPTER 15

JUDGES *and* JURIES

You shall appoint judges and officers in all your gates, which the LORD your God gives you, according to your tribes, and they shall judge the people with just judgment. You shall not pervert justice; you shall not show partiality, nor take a bribe, for a bribe blinds the eyes of the wise and twists the words of the righteous. You shall follow what is altogether just, that you may live and inherit the land which the LORD your God is giving you.

DEUTERONOMY 16:18–20

W e must consider another variation on "by their tactics ye shall know them." When controversy erupts in a church, and it is over the color of the carpet in the nursery, the end result can be a personal and ecclesiastical mess. But when the stakes are higher, it is not rare for the civil magistrate to get involved. And when this happens, it is almost always the result of at least one party in the dispute ignoring the apostle Paul's teaching in 1 Corinthians 6. In that (very *clear*) passage, the apostle Paul prohibits Christians from going before unbelieving adjudicatories to have their disputes sorted out. And by "prohibits" we mean to indicate that Paul teaches that Christians, to use the theological phrase, *may not do it.*

We must note in the first place that this does not mean that two believers cannot have their dispute resolved by a civil magistrate. He says clearly that the problem is *not* that it is a civil authority handling the matter. The problem is unbelief. In the first verse, Paul reacts to Christians taking a matter to law "before the unrighteous" instead of bringing it before the saints. In the second verse, he makes a dichotomy between the world and the saints. And in the sixth verse, he clinches the matter by saying in disgust that brother goes to law against brother, and "that before unbelievers." This means that if we postulate a Christian republic, biblical laws, a Christian judge, and a property line dispute between two Christians, there would be no disgrace in having the civil magistrate settle the matter. In that case, there would an ungodly usurpation of authority if the church tried to intervene and settle the matter. Property line disputes are not within the ordinary jurisdiction of the church—although Paul tells believers to have such disputes settled there in an *ad hoc* way rather than to take the dispute before unbelievers.

One other limitation should be noted. Paul is talking about lawsuits and complaints of that order (*pragma* is the word). This restriction does not apply to calling the cops in cases of murder, rape, or grand theft auto. If someone is peeling out of your driveway in your new car, you need not have a family discussion over the likelihood of the thief being a baptized Christian before you call the cops.

Moreover, having sought to settle the dispute privately, and presuming there is evidence to support your claim of a wrong having been perpetrated against you, you certainly can bring the matter to the church for resolution. "Is it so, that there is not a wise man among you, not even one, who will be able to judge between his brethren?" (1 Cor. 6:5). The church could be involved in this in a variety of ways, formally or informally. If one party refuses to submit to the church's judgment, either by being unwilling to have the church settle the matter or by refusing to abide by the settlement they call for, we now have a different situation. If one party, in either of these cases, then proceeds to the unbelieving civil court for remedy, the church now has an idea of who's who in the dispute, and the option of some form of church discipline might be called for.

So we are talking about disputes, lawsuits, did-too-did-nots, and the like. In our day, we have a system of civil law that is secular—formally and judicially unbelieving. The apostle Paul clearly lays down the law here. Do *not* take disputes between Christians before them. One response to this would obviously be, from one of the parties, "But I was *wronged*. If I do as you say, I will have to pay the costs of being defrauded." And Paul shows how strongly he feels about this when he says that our response should be to willingly embrace that loss rather than to disgrace the

Church by airing our dirty laundry in front of unbelievers. If you have to eat it, Paul says, then eat it (v. 7).

Paul assumes here that it is quite possible that one Christian has wronged another, and he assumes that it is not wrong for the innocent party to complain, or for his complaint to be adjudicated within the Church. But he declares that the wronged party, *for the sake of the Church's testimony*, should be willing to be defrauded instead of appealing to unbelievers for relief. And notice that he does not set a dollar amount on when this willingness to be ripped off should cease.

For those who read the Bible in a straightforward and honest way, the matter is therefore settled. But if a man has a lot of money on the line (or if he is emotionally cantankerous), he will be tempted to get into a few Greek word studies. There is a marvelous phrase in the *Westminster Confession*, talking about divorce, that says men are apt to "study arguments." Time for a little creative exegesis!

Now it is quite possible for a Christian who was truly wronged to fall into this temptation, especially if the wrong was significant or high-handed. But when there is a reflex action that turns to the unbelieving civil authorities readily and easily, and produces strained arguments for doing it *without blushing*, this tells you something immediately about the spiritual state of that individual and the spiritual state of everyone who sides with him.

Say that a couple of Christians in the same church have a property line dispute, and they cannot come to an agreement. After their second (short) discussion, one of them takes the matter to court in high disregard of Paul's instruction here. The other settles, rather than appear in court, allowing himself to lose. He loses rather than fighting in front of the unbelievers. Now in an ordinary matter like this, it would be very easy for us to assume that it was the guilty party who "settled" rather than being fully accountable. But in this scenario, it is quite possible that it should go the other way. What does high-handed disobedience of the Scriptures by one of the parties tell you about him? It tells you that he clearly doesn't care what the Bible says about handling and processing disputes. So why should he care what the Bible says about the dispute itself?

Put this another way. When a private dispute boils out into the streets, and you were not there when the dispute began, can you make any assessment at all? Well, sure, at least enough to get oriented. The fight is now going on in front of you, and if one of the parties is fighting dirty right in front of you, you are allowed to consider the possibility that he was fighting dirty before you laid eyes on him. And if the other party is fighting clean, then that should be significant also. Now, considering everything else we have said about justice, these considerations must be weighed together with all the other scriptural criteria. But if you are watching a fight, and there is bitterness and rancor on one side, and self-restraint and honor on the other, this is not insignificant. And dragging a fight before

unbelievers displays a win-at-all-costs mentality that is a
prime example of fighting dirty.

Over the last few years we have seen multiple examples
of this kind of thing. Disputes that professing Christians
have with other Christians have repeatedly been dragged
before various unbelieving adjudicatories—commissions,
city councils, courts, and so on. Not only have the deeply disgruntled done this, they have not been challenged
on this overt disobedience by others who have publicly
gathered by their side in support. So they gather together,
filing complaints and briefs, and in various other ways,
figuring out ways to humiliate the apostle. Of course, they
would not say that this is what they are doing. That is because they have "studied arguments."

WITH WOOLLY MITTENS ON

Watching church conflicts from a distance is like watching a water polo game—much of what constitutes the
actual game is not happening above the surface where
you can see it from the back row. You can tell when the
ball goes in the goal, but what you don't actually see are
the three pair of swimming trunks on the bottom of the
pool. There is a reason we don't place the referees in the
back rows of the stadium. You can't see from there, and
shouldn't be asked to. But to continue the sports analogy,
there are (occasional) times when everyone in the stadium
sees a flagrant foul, and the referee misses it. However,
most of the time, we place the referees in the midst of the

action because that is the best place to make the necessary determinations. And after every play, we do not form a committee of the whole. We do not have a review of the call and invite all the fans who want to contribute their two cents to come down on the field and look at the replay, too.

So those who are charged with sorting these things out hold an important office in the church. In the course of doing this, elders are not only permitted to keep information with discretion and appropriate confidentiality, they are *charged* to do this. They have been duly ordained to rule over the church for a reason, having been tested, approved and installed into an authoritative office. They know their people, including background and things that are not public knowledge. They are privy to evidence that others have no access to. In fact, they often know things about people and cases that they may not reveal to the onlookers. If they did so, they would be violating their office. This confidentiality expectation is sometimes used by people who know that the pastor or elders cannot defend themselves.

As mentioned earlier, there have always been gunslingers who are gunning for the big guy (that's a relative term—if you're a little man, then everyone seems big). A variety of things might motivate this aggressive behavior: hatred of authority, father hunger, bitterness, wanting to make a name for oneself, arrogance, pride, etc. Regardless of the motive, there are apparently folks who take some pleasure in bringing someone down. Perhaps it is like see-ing a guy in a dunking-booth—irresistible.

These "troublers of Israel" have little regard for the col-lateral damage they cause to the church. The peace and purity of the church is of little concern to them. For some reason, what they really want is to trash someone's reputa-tion, and when it comes to emptying their bottles of vitri-ol, they do not stint. They do this by lying, by anonymous accusation, by slander, and by any other means that occur to them. Moreover, if they can get two other parties to shoot it out, that will save them the trouble of being shot at themselves. "Did you hear what he called you? Are you going to put up with that?"

If we are dealing with a "Jimmy Swaggart and the prostitute" kind of situation, and the whole nation is aware of it, then discussion of it could be edifying, and it could well be obscurantism not to discuss it. But if we are dealing with accusations of that kind of behavior made by people who are ashamed of their real names . . . To try to deal with such situations at internet speeds and distances is like trying to paint a fine watercolor with your thumbs. With wooly mittens on.

In most cases, the folks who hear a church's public ex-planation of a matter can usually be divided into three cat-egories. There are, in the first place, those who understand what we're trying to say. If they are foolish enough to say this publicly, they are then categorized as groupies and cultists. Then there are those who will never understand what we're trying to say because they have their skivvies in a serious twist over the matter. Don't even try to answer those who are only and always interested in more ammo. The third category would be those who really would accept a full explanation if it were laid out completely, but for various reasons, it strikes them that we're being mysteriously coy.

When a situation is analyzed from thirty thousand feet, it is easy to base what you see in it on presuppositions that are largely unquestioned and invisible. A few data points are all you have, and your mind inevitably wants to connect those dots and fill in the gaps. We can make assumptions about all kinds of things that we are in no position to know or judge. In fact, ninety-eight percent of the data may in fact be missing while you simultaneously presume that you possess ninety-eight percent of the relevant information. When looking at a situation from the outside, a charitable judgment is called for (e.g., a presumption of innocence). Perhaps you don't know as much about the situation as you think you do. Moreover, those who are in a position to know are not always at liberty to say. Some matters are private, confidential, and might be harmful to other innocent parties. Not everything that can be said should be said.

One of the reasons there are high standards for church office is the fact that such officers will be in possession of sensitive information, information that can, if misused, hurt folks. This is why it is important to carefully select those who will hold these offices, because a high degree of trust is called for. It is also why having more than one such man is critical (e.g., a session of elders). When important matters of justice are placed in their hands, the parties involved are relying on their honest work. While it might be appropriate, under some circumstances, to make inquiry as to what is being done to rectify a certain situation, it is not always appropriate for those in authority to reveal all that has been said and done. In fact, in most cases a large part of the information should not be revealed.

If we know the men who are making the judgments, and if we trust them, then we should be content (having seen their families and known their commitment to the Word of God). Ministry is impossible (even in a good-sized local church) unless you farm things like this out. And this is why the Bible places such a high premium on the *character* of elders and pastors. You simply cannot know the details of every situation, so you need to be sure that a certain kind of man is entrusted with sorting out the various situations that arise. We back these men of integrity. When you trust someone to make a determination on your behalf, it is like that person is writing a check on the account he has with you. Godly men make deposits in our accounts frequently during the good times, so that when the times of trouble come, they are in a position to make withdrawals. Their credit exceeds their expenditures. We trust them, and for reasons that the Bible describes as the basis for trusting men in ministry.

There are public sins that must be dealt with publicly, but not every accusation against a leader rises to this level. When accusations are brought against anyone, it is crucial for all potential participants, witnesses, or observers to think of the matter biblically. This is because it is perilously easy to fall into that species of harmful do-goodism that wants to uproot the tares, but that kind of do-goodism is diabolical.

This is true of accusations of private wrongdoing (e.g., embezzlement) and accusations of public heresy. We have already shown that the two need to be handled differently, according to Scripture. The first should be handled by the elders of the people, who conduct a careful investigation (Deut. 19). The second, as a public matter, should be handled as a public matter in public view (Jesus said to ask the people what He taught). But even with this difference acknowledged, there is still a common element in both situations that everyone should be aware of.

First, we need to see that—from Genesis to Revelation—the godly prosecutor has a paucity of role models. The overall theme of the Scripture is that the true conservatives are the falsely *accused*; it is one of the great ironies of our day that ostensible conservatives want to earn their gunslinging stripes by *accusing*. Think of it: Abel accused by Cain, Joseph accused by his brothers and by Potiphar's wife, David accused by Saul, Jeremiah accused by the court prophets, and of course the Lord Jesus accused by the Sanhedrin. Where in Scripture is the theme of the zealous accuser who wants to root out some troublemaker?

There are some—Joshua with Achan, or Josiah with the idolaters of Israel. But the words *Satan* and *devil*, with their deep connotations of adversarial accusation, are used as they are for a reason.

This is no argument against church government or lawful church discipline. It is merely a cautionary note—those who have been entrusted with authority in the church need to take as their top priority an ecclesiastical version of the Hippocratic oath—"First, do no harm." Those who bring charges lawfully need to do so with fear and trembling and with a profound awareness of how often charges have been brought in the course of Scripture and in the history of the church by those who *thought* they were serving God.

The great Puritan Thomas Watson said that it is better to be wronged than to do wrong. It is not a sin to *be* wronged. Those who are in a position to do wrong (with authority) need to make a point of going the extra mile to put this understanding into practice. The Lord Jesus said that all manner of blasphemy against *Him* would be forgiven, but that the sin against the Holy Spirit would not be (Matt. 12:31–32). This means, among other things, that those who in their calling and vocation are representing the Lord Jesus (ministers) ought to be like the Lord in this. This is why in our practice we have disciplined those who have abandoned their spouses, for example, but have been very slow to discipline those who rail against us. God sees, and He will sort that kind of thing out.

There are some who are distressed on our behalf over the lies that are being told about us. But this is just part of the cost of doing business. Jesus said to expect it and to rejoice when it happened, and Scripture requires those in spiritual authority to take care that they not react in a manner that makes the accusations retroactively true. False accusations of tyranny could provoke a man into tyranny.

The last thing in the world that elders and pastors should want is the perception that they are using the apparatus of justice to sandbag their own position. Church discipline should be obviously the kind of thing that has the health of the whole body in mind. Now because of the overarching theme of the Bible, and because of the great moral force of Christ's example on the cross, this explains why, in our contemporary disputes, everyone needs to be the accused. This is where playing the victim comes from. The victims of course want to be the victims, which is their right. There *are* true victims. But prosecutors, persecutors, slanderers, liemongers, accusers, and all their cousins *also* need to be the victim. This explains why, if someone lies about me, and I laugh at it, in their minds I have committed a mortal offense against public decency. Our sympathies go out to these people—it is really hard to be the accuser and the victim at the same time.

In a public matter, such as a trial, interested folks should acquaint themselves with the available facts. When the accused proclaims his innocence and allows himself to be examined and cross-examined in a public forum, then

we have an opportunity and an obligation to inform ourselves. If, for example, a minister is accused of false teaching, then he usually will have a trail of sermons, lectures,
writings, etc. by which he can be known. Reading through
this material or listening to the audio is not to side with
the accused or his accusers. It is to acquaint yourself with
what is going on, and when you do this, you are in a position to do so as a friend of justice. As Paul said to Agrippa,
these things were not done in a corner.

CHAPTER 16

CONSCIENCE
and COURAGE

*To the pure all things are pure, but to those who are defiled
and unbelieving nothing is pure; but even their mind and
conscience are defiled.*

TITUS 1:15

I n the course of controversy, due consideration
must be given to those who get caught in the
crossfire. The Westminster Confession of Faith
says that God alone is Lord of the conscience, and this is
not just talking about those consciences that are rightly
informed. We tend to understand this principle on some
subjects—there are many issues where we are told in
Scripture to leave the sensitive conscience alone, and this
presupposes that the sensitive conscience is too scrupulous. Now people can have conscience issues about all
kinds of things—dress, food, reading, entertainment—
and this is the kind of thing the apostle Paul addresses
in the latter part of Romans.

But people can also have conscience issues based on controversies, rumors, and stuff they read on the internet. And, as in the earlier cases, their consciences can be ill-informed. Say that someone is invited to visit a certain church somewhere in the country, and they decline to do so. The reason for this is not because they know anything for certain, but rather because they are nervous over stuff they have heard. The rumors and suspicions are enough to make attending such a church a conscience issue for this individual. He wants to stay as far away from the potential controversies as he can, which in itself is a noble sentiment.

What are we to do with such an individual? Well, nothing. We bless him and ask God to keep him and make His face to shine upon him. Whether or not he should have been so skeptical about things he heard, whether or not he has understood the biblical principles of justice, he honestly holds to what he does, and his conscience is to be *honored* and treated with respect. This means that we are called to honor certain opinions (as honestly held) that might reflect poorly on us. And we shouldn't really want to argue about it. If we stick our head through the canvas in a booth at the county fair, we can't really be surprised if people throw wet sponges at it. What this boils down to is the undeniable reality that there are *godly* Christian people out there who think that some other Christians are dangerous. They don't feel like investigating; they don't want to check; the instinctive *blech* is sufficient. Depending on how they got there, God bless them all.

But in Scripture, deference to conscience is always to a tender conscience. Consider this defense: "You can't make me stop what I am doing because I really think it, and my conscience is set." If we apply what is argued above, then does this not make the city of conscience the all-purpose city of refuge? Do whatever you want, say whatever you want, slander however you want, and then scurry off to the altar of conscience and grab its horns like Joab? Jeremiah Burroughs makes a helpful observation on how to deal with those who want to make "conscience" the universal trump card—he makes a distinction between the tender conscience and the turbulent conscience. "If a man is proud and turbulent in his carriage, by that you may know the devil is rather in the will than in the conscience. Though an erroneous conscience may cause one to hold fast an error, yet it does not cause proud, scornful, turbulent behavior."[1]

Differences of opinion can be *conscientiously* held by men in fellowship with the Father. But it is *not* possible to be conscientiously turbulent and arrogantly scornful. The thing that is necessary is for conscientious men who have a legitimate role to play in a situation to work diligently at *respecting* all the principal parties involved. The one thing we know at the outset is that to the extent they deal with conscience at all, turbulent blogs are places that sear them.

Adding to Burroughs's observation, not only should we summarily dismiss the turbulent as having nothing

1. Burroughs, 45.

constructive to offer, we should also warn those who use
the turbulent agitators in a good cop/bad cop kind of
way. They don't themselves heave any Jell-O in the junior
high cafeteria food fight, but they encourage and cheer on
those who do. "Good shot, Raymond!" They refuse to sign
on to the *entire* agenda of Turbulence.com, but they do
think that some legitimate points "have been raised there"
and so they "want answers."

Sorry. Answers are for responsible people.

REAL COURAGE

It is understandable that, for a variety of reasons, many
want to give a wide berth to a given controversy. Perhaps
it doesn't interest them, or it interests them only mildly.
Every fight is not your fight, so the sidelines are the place
to be. But being on the sidelines is not the same as being
in the peanut gallery, enjoying the circus for the sake of
the show, lurking for Jesus. Athletes play the game; couch
potatoes observe the game, rooting for their team and
complaining about the referees. It takes courage to suit up.

The pursuit of truth and justice is not for the faint of
heart. Whether it involves a personal conflict, an ecclesiastical conflict, or a civil conflict, there are many points
where the temptation to cave in or retreat is significant. It
takes real courage to fight for justice. No good deed goes
unpunished. Parents, pastors, and judges can be, and often are, cowards in the face of conflict. Political pressures
are brought to bear, and they capitulate. But courageous

parents, pastors, and judges, in the face of the same kinds of pressures, stand firm; they don't back down. The pursuit of justice can be costly, and it is likely that in the end somebody, or some group of somebodies, will not be happy with what they have done. True justice is not determined by popular vote.

The courageous know what fear is, but they do what is right in the face of that fear. Cowards, in the face of the same fear, hide out. They, however, usually have no shortage of opinions as to what *others* ought to be doing; they're brave with other people's lives and reputations. Conflict and justice involve risks. In a fallen world, the pursuit of justice sometimes requires warfare, which, inevitably, requires getting shot at.

CHAPTER 17

THE SUPREME COURT

*Repay no one evil for evil. Have regard for good things in
the sight of all men. If it is possible, as much as depends on
you, live peaceably with all men. Beloved, do not avenge
yourselves, but rather give place to wrath; for it is written,
"Vengeance is Mine, I will repay," says the Lord.*

ROMANS 12:17–49

A s we pursue justice in the midst of a tangle, the temptation to want to *assist* the process can be strong. We desire immediate justice, and when we feel that it is eluding us, our urge to execute justice on our own terms can be strong. This is especially so when we are the objects of the injustice. But justice is not always achieved by Thursday. It might not be achieved next year, or in our lifetime, but court has not adjourned. In due time, all accounts will be settled.

We must never forget that there is a final judgment and justice: "Beloved, do not avenge yourselves, but rather give place to wrath; for it is written, 'Vengeance is Mine, I will repay,' says the Lord" (Rom. 12:19). "And as it is

appointed for men to die once, but after this the judgment" (Heb. 9:27). "The Lord knows how to deliver the
godly out of temptations and to reserve the unjust under
punishment for the day of judgment, and especially those
who walk according to the flesh in the lust of uncleanness
and despise authority" (2 Pet. 2:9–10).

The omniscient judge of the universe will dispense
perfect justice. The guilty must be dealt with one way
or the other. The righteous will be exonerated and their
names will be cleared. The Scriptures give us much instruction in these matters: "Be sure your sin will find
you out" (Num. 32:23). "Do not be deceived, God is not
mocked; for whatever a man sows, that he will also reap.
For he who sows to his flesh will of the flesh reap corruption, but he who sows to the Spirit will of the Spirit
reap everlasting life. And let us not grow weary while
doing good, for in due season we shall reap if we do not
lose heart" (Gal. 6:7–9). "The mouth of the righteous
speaks wisdom, and his tongue talks of justice. The law
of his God is in his heart; none of his steps shall slide.
The wicked watches the righteous, and seeks to slay him.
The LORD will not leave him in his hand, nor condemn
him when he is judged. Wait on the LORD, and keep His
way, and He shall exalt you to inherit the land; when the
wicked are cut off, you shall see it" (Ps. 37:30–34). "For
He is coming to judge the earth. With righteousness He
shall judge the world, and the peoples with equity" (Ps.
98:9). And so on.

Divine justice is far greater than mere legal justice. It thoroughly vindicates the righteous. It thoroughly exposes sin and wickedness. It does so with an infallible application of an infallible standard. Temporary wrongs will be made right. "Now therefore, it is already an utter failure for you that you go to law against one another. Why do you not rather accept wrong? Why do you not rather let yourselves be cheated?" (1 Cor. 6:7). "Therefore humble yourselves under the mighty hand of God, that He may exalt you in due time, casting all your care upon Him, for He cares for you" (1 Pet. 5:6–7). "Oh, love the LORD, all you His saints! For the LORD preserves the faithful, and fully repays the proud person. Be of good courage, and He shall strengthen your heart, all you who hope in the LORD" (Ps. 31:23–24).

However, there is frequently a foretaste of eternal justice in the temporal realm. We sometimes call this poetic justice. "So they hanged Haman on the gallows that he had prepared for Mordecai" (Esther 7:10). "The nations have sunk down in the pit which they made; in the net which they hid, their own foot is caught. The LORD is known by the judgment He executes; the wicked is snared in the work of his own hands" (Ps. 9:15–16).

Following all the biblical guidelines for justice still might not yield the immediate justice a person wants. Sometime the unjust do, temporarily, "get away." Sometimes, the innocent are left unsatisfied. But the trial is never over until God has spoken, and He will speak.

Sometime He speaks next week, or next year, or next decade, but when it comes to the guilty, their foot will slide.

The Bible describes some obvious judgments from God executed against the guilty: Adam and Eve, those outside the ark, Sodom and Gomorrah, Korah's rebellion, Ananias and Sapphira, and many more. Yet there are also many not-so-obvious judgments executed, as well. Absalom's "accident," the suicide of Judas, and God's giving up to vile passions those who received "in themselves the penalty of their error which was due," (Rom. 1:24, 27). Their own devices "became a snare to them" (Ps. 106:36).

MERCY, FORGIVENESS, AND GRACE

Injustice is, of course, not new to our generation; it's as old as the devil. Many have been hurt and even ruined by the malicious, careless and unjust accusations of others. Caught up in a conflict or controversy, hasty and ill-informed actors thrust their swords with little regard for justice. Iain Murray cites an example of this in his biography of Jonathan Edwards, describing situation at Edwards's church in North Hampton, a place where he had faithfully served for many years. Edwards was on the receiving end of false accusations and slanders (in the midst of a controversy), by factions who had their own agendas. These were led, in part, by a disaffected cousin, Joseph Hawley, Jr. Nearly four years later, Hawley wrote a letter of repentance to Edwards in August 1754. Murray says, "Hawley's sorrow was such that he was not satisfied until, in May 1760, a letter from him to Edwards's friend, David Hall, was published in a Boston newspaper."[1] This letter is a picture of what unabashed repentance looks like, and it is the prelude to mercy, forgiveness, and grace, all of which were extended to Hawley by Edwards. This was published, making his repentance public:

> In the course of that most melancholy contention with Mr. Edwards, I now see that I was very much influenced by vast pride, self-sufficiency, ambition, and vanity. I appear to myself vile, and doubtless much more so to others who are more impartial . . . Such treatment of Mr. Edwards, wherein I was so deeply concerned and active, was particularly and very aggravatedly sinful and ungrateful in me, because I was not only under the common obligations of each individual of the society to him, as a most able, diligent and faithful pastor; but I had also received many instances of his tenderness, goodness and generosity to me as a young kinsman, whom he was disposed to treat in a most friendly manner . . . I am most sorely sensible that nothing but that infinite grace and mercy which saved some of the betrayers and murderers of our blessed Lord, and the persecutors of his martyrs, can pardon me; in which alone I hope for pardon, for the sake of Christ, whose blood, blessed be God, cleanseth from all sin.[2]

1. Iain H. Murray, *Jonathan Edwards: A New Biography* (Carlisle, PA: The Banner of Truth Trust, 1987), 348.
2. Murray, 348.

In the Bible, mercy often follows justice, but justice must precede mercy. Justice might come in the form of a defendant pleading guilty and throwing himself on the mercy of the court. It might also come when an individual confesses guilt and receives the forgiveness of the offended. Someone has to pay for the sin; either the sinner himself or the person sinned against. The unrepentant sinner has no place to go without confession. "Be sure, your sins will find you out" (Num. 32:23). God will by no means clearing the guilty (Exod. 34:7). Jesus "bore our sins in His body on the tree" (1 Pet. 2:24); He did this first, so that forgiveness and mercy could then be extended to us. But such forgiveness is always preceded by confession (1 John 1:9). The one sinned against picks up the tab.

In any case—civil, ecclesiastical, or familial; formal or informal—justice is the initial goal. Mercy and forgiveness might follow, but they can only follow when genuine justice is first made plain. The role of the prosecution is not simply to make an accusation, but also to deliver the necessary *credible proof* to substantiate the charges and achieve justice. Likewise, the role of a defender is not necessarily to "help someone beat the charges," but rather to insure a just trial and a just result. Both the accuser and the accused might have certain prejudices in the matter, but those in legitimate positions to adjudicate the matter must weigh all things if justice is to be rendered. After justice, then there is the possibility of mercy; then the mercy has value.

The name *Satan* not only means *accuser* but is also related to the word for *slander*. The devil is the accuser of the brethren; he accuses day and night. When the sons of God were gathering in the presence of God, God bragged on His servant Job, and Satan was the one who accused him of false motives. This father of lies is filled with false accusations, and there is a fallen world filled with his offspring.

We call Jesus by the name Jesus because He will save His people from their sins. Jesus is an advocate for us, a defense attorney. And He is not an advocate for the innocent. "And if any man sin, we have an advocate with the Father, Jesus Christ the Righteous" (1 John 2:1). Note that it is *righteous* for God to defend those who have sinned in this fashion. Jesus is Immanuel, God with us. He was born of a woman, born under law, so that those living in darkness could see a great light. He became incarnate so that we might have comfort. And when Jesus was preparing His disciples for His time of departure, He promised them that He would send the Holy Spirit as His own replacement. The Holy Spirit is called the Comforter, the Encourager, the *Paraclete*.

There is a chasm between these two mentalities. The chasm is so great that once we begin to understand it, we need to begin assembling careful arguments from Scripture to allow for a Christian to serve as a prosecutor or accuser. There are such arguments, and there is an appropriate or godly way to fill such necessary roles in our society. We do have a need for prosecuting attorneys. But we need to know where the warnings are. It is like wealth. The Bible has a tremendous amount to say on the subject of wealth, and much of it consists of *warnings*. It is lawful to have wealth, but watch yourself. It is lawful, in a similar way, to become an accuser. But if a man does, he has to know that he is stepping into a role that appears to have stumbled the devil himself. Don't be a fool who rushes in where angels fear to tread.

The "very concerned" often have a false sense of their own moral superiority. C.S. Lewis observed, "Of all tyrannies a tyranny sincerely exercised for the good of its victim may be the most oppressive. It may be better to live under robber barons than under omnipotent moral busybodies. The robber baron's cruelty may sometimes sleep, his cupidity may at some point be satiated, but those who torment us for our own good will torment us without end for they do so with the approval of their own conscience."[3]

Christians need to learn how to repent of their *virtues*. Our vices are easy enough to identify as displeasing to God, but our virtues really get underfoot. This is one of them: Righteous indignation is one of the besetting sins of those who believe themselves to be moral when they are merely moralistic. This is why Jesus said that a time would come when those viciously attacking the church would believe that they were doing a service to God. The mentality of the persecutor is one of serene self-confidence because it

3. C.S. Lewis, *God in the Dock: Essays on Theology* (Grand Rapids: Eerdmans, 1972), 292.

is self-evident to him that sin must always be *accused*. But for those who are thinking biblically, sin makes us think of our need for a Savior, a Defender, an Advocate.

Another way of saying all this is that the Christian faith declares to the world salvation by grace. A zeal for the grace of God, Scripture teaches, is a zeal for righteousness. If we confess our sins, John says, God is faithful *and just* to forgive us our sins. This is a righteousness that goes all the way down to bedrock. In stark contrast to this, the Bible teaches us to see the righteousness of the muckraker as a tin sheet righteousness, nailed in a cock-eyed way to the dilapidated shed of self-improvement.

CHAPTER 18

JUSTICE *and*
SEX ABUSE

Great and marvelous are Your works,
Lord God Almighty!
Just and true are Your ways,
O King of the saints!

REVELATION 15:3

I n this chapter we are going to be dealing with the problem created by registered sex offenders attending church. However, before we get there, we want to say something about the cultural context we find ourselves in. And that said, we want to warn you beforehand that the point we are going to draw from that context is probably not what you think we are going to draw.

When God created man in His image, He created them male and female. Their unique sexual identity was given to be a powerful blessing (Prov. 5:18), not only to them, but also to the world ("be fruitful and multiply" Gen. 1:28; "godly offspring" Mal. 2:15). This was part of the creation that God pronounced to be "good" (Gen. 2:18). Sex was an extremely powerful tool for fulfilling the good task that God gave to man and woman. Sin changed the game. Sex retained its power, but now it had the ability not only to create lives, but also to destroy lives. The number of sexual sins and perversions began to multiply, and the corruption spread. None of us are untainted: "None are righteous, no not one." Some of those sexual sins rose to the level of crimes. Some of them were even capital crimes (Rom. 1:32), because they were a threat to the lives of individuals, families, and societies.

When a culture doesn't know God, or abandons the God it once knew, anything and everything is up for grabs. At that point, sexuality has no boundaries except those that are arbitrarily adopted. If there is no God—if it is simply a matter of survival of the fittest—then the arbitrary borders of sexual ethics are constantly shifting. There can be no forbidden fruit. Everyone does what is right in their own eyes. The society becomes schizophrenic, wanting to be liberated from all constraints (Ps. 2:3), while recognizing that with complete anarchy the party will soon be over. Thus an oversexualized or pornified culture can act shocked and outraged when its worldview of sexual abandon spills over toward children. Abercrombie and Fitch can market baby panties with the words "eye candy" printed on the bottom, television can fill our homes with images of sexualized children, the unfettered internet can constantly be in the palm of every child, and then we can all act shocked and outraged when someone actually acts out one of these sexual fantasies on an eight-year-old. No doubt, child sexual abuse is as old as the hills. This fire has been burning for a long time, but we have now filled the world with gas cans. We feed the fire and then act surprised when people get burned. The sin of child sex abuse is an individual sin, but it is also one of society's sins. There is plenty of culpability to go around.

But there must remain some point of outrage even in a world that has gone mad, and having mainstreamed so many other outrages, it now takes pedophilia to really offend our sense of decency. "We're not barbarians. We do have our limits. Put the monsters away. They're not like us." Now the Bible agrees that, in many cases, such crimes are horrific and that we should "put away from ourselves the evil person" (Deut. 22:25–27; 1 Cor. 5:13). Hand them over to God for perfect justice and for the protection of children and families and societies. But again, our schizophrenic world is both kinder than God (with no death penalty or church discipline), and more cruel than God (warehousing men in cages for twenty years) and then releasing them with a "scarlet letter" (registered sex offender) for the rest of their lives. (I thought only the Puritans did such things!) If the state would administer biblical justice, then many of the other dilemmas we face would be taken care of.

We are not suggesting that the criminal courts should not be involved in the administration of true justice in

cases of genuine sexual abuse; of course they should.
Criminals should turn themselves in or be turned over.
Unfortunately, the justice system is often unjust in both
directions. Justice should be neither too harsh nor too lenient. God's word is the standard for personal ethics and
for criminal justice. We welcome a wise application of that
standard across the board.

A PORNIFIED CULTURE

There is no way to pornify a culture the way we have done
without making porn far more available to kids than it
used to be. And kids obviously learn from what they see.
This includes what we call mainstream entertainment,
not just the triple-X stuff. We now have young kids who
have seen, or who have heard about on the playground,
practices that previous generations learned about in their
second year of med school. Nobody should be surprised
when some junior high boy tries out some of what he has
seen or heard about on his younger sister. When sexual
corruption becomes ubiquitous, many more kids are going
to get swept up in it. Call it the collateral damage of the
sexual revolution.

But we are not saying this in any exculpatory way.
Corruption is corruption, and being steeped in corruption
from childhood does not remove any personal responsibility. We are a sinful race. So this point has nothing
to do with the making of excuses for the perpetrators of
sex crimes—while it is true that many victimizers were

victims themselves first, that doesn't make any of it right. Personal responsibility is assigned by the Bible, and not by our experiences.

So why make the point about pornification then? Well, it should be obvious that those who promote and advance such corruptions of a sexual nature in one area ought not to be entrusted with adjudication of crimes and offenses of a sexual nature in another area. In many cases our establishment no longer knows what sex itself is supposed to be and so cannot know what sexual justice is supposed to be. We therefore ought not to rely on their "wisdom" about sexual justice as it relates to children. They frequently have forfeited that wisdom. Our cultural milieu tolerates and teaches courses in our universities which solemnly maintain that all instances of PIV (penis in vagina) are rape by definition, dogmatically pronounce that TMI sex education for grade schoolers is a moral necessity, say that doing the anal honors should be considered a high privilege, and now with same sex-mirage having received the supremes' judicial blessing, has already been preparing to mainstream pedophilia. The last thing in the world Christians should do is join in with any stampeding opinions about any of this from the secularists.

Many of them don't know what sex is for, and they therefore don't know what sexual justice is. Here is (just) one example of secularist dogma that Christians are bound to reject: "Sex offenders don't ever change." This is not only an error, it is an error which strikes at the heart of the gospel's efficacy. Now it is quite true that sex offenders don't ever change *themselves*, but this is true for the same reason that thieves and adulterers never change *themselves*. Christ came into the world to save sinners, including the really messed up ones.

"Know ye not that the unrighteous shall not inherit the kingdom of God? Be not deceived: neither fornicators, nor idolaters, nor adulterers, nor effeminate, nor abusers of themselves with mankind, Nor thieves, nor covetous, nor drunkards, nor revilers, nor extortioners, shall inherit the kingdom of God. And such were some of you: but ye are washed, but ye are sanctified, but ye are justified in the name of the Lord Jesus, and by the Spirit of our God" (1 Cor. 6:9–11). The words translated here as *effeminate and abusers of themselves with mankind* refer to homosexual behavior, plainly and unambiguously. (Anyone who says otherwise is blowing some scholarly smoke at you.) And who does not know that, in the ancient world, this kind of practice routinely included young boys? But our point in citing this passage is not to prove that this kind of behavior is immoral, as much as that point might be needed in other discussions, but rather to demonstrate that "sex offenders cannot change" is a lie straight out of the pit of hell. Among the Corinthians, do you think there were any converts who had been given over fully to the ancient ways with a whole series of young boys? *"And such were some of you: but ye are washed, but ye are sanctified, but ye are justified in the name of the Lord Jesus, and by the Spirit of our God."*

Thus, if a sex offender is kept outside the congregation and is served communion in a back room, then what you are actually doing is making a liturgical statement that he ought not be served communion at all. If he is vile, and cannot change, then excommunicate him and be done with it. Your justification for such excommunication would then have to be that "such people never change." But if he can repent and be brought to the Table, then he must be brought to the Table with all the other forgiven sinners—which perhaps includes the rest of us. Of all places, we must remember at the Table that he is part of the church—we must discern the body (1 Cor. 11:29) and acknowledge that he is a member of it.

But, of course . . . the fact that repentant sex offenders can repent and can be truly forgiven does not mean that a particular individual's professed repentance is genuine. We are not required to live in la-la land. Forgiveness and trust are two very different things, so when a convicted sex offender is brought into fellowship with the rest of the congregation, it must be done in such a way that no parent has any reasonable cause to be worried about what could happen. Forgiveness doesn't mean that a registered sex offender is made a Sunday School teacher any more than a convicted embezzler is made the church treasurer. And one of the ways true repentance is manifested is that the person involved is not at all offended by this necessity and understands completely that although his sin is forgiven, certain consequences necessarily remain. Paul once said that if he had been guilty of anything deserving of death, he did not refuse to die (Acts 25:11). A repentant offender receives the consequences, and, as much as possible, is eager to have the consequences of his crimes fall on himself.

If a known criminal presents himself to the church, he should be called to repentance, and part of that repentance is to turn himself in. If he will not, then we should not only question his repentance, but we should report him to the appropriate legal authorities. The protection of the innocent is the highest priority. The redemption of the guilty is a close second. But what if that criminal has just been released from doing his time, and he cannot be turned over to anyone? He professes to have come to know Jesus through a prison ministry and now wants to unite with a good church in order to continue with his sanctification in Christ. The church cannot execute him and has no power to further imprison him. Our mission of redemption is the same for him as it is for every other sinner. "The gospel of Christ, for it is the power of God to salvation for everyone who believes" (Rom. 1:16). What shall we do?

As pastors, we have been lied to by the best of them; manipulation abounds, con men on every corner. A profession of faith is a good start, but it is not sufficient. Caution and skepticism are part of wisdom. Trust but verify. A repentant man is a humble man. In instances of sexual abuse, he has violated the trust of everyone and it is likely that (in serious cases) trust will never be fully restored.

Trust and forgiveness are not the same thing. Forgiveness is not earned, it is granted. Trust must be earned.

Since the protection of the innocent is of the first order, a range of appropriate limitations must be placed on such a person. This is not uncommon with other sins (e.g., substance abuse, adultery, theft). We will not try to list all the possible protections that could be put in place (each case and circumstance would call for different rules). Nevertheless, such limitations would likely include informing the congregation, personal supervision, restricted movements, ongoing counseling, and whatever else is necessary to insure the safety of all parties. What it would not include is separate worship and communion services.

If a repentant sex offender were received into the church as a true follower of Jesus Christ, then he would not only have a place at the Table of the Lord, he would also be welcome to join in the communion of the saints, with the saints. Public worship and public communion are the places for all redeemed sinners. This would likely require the shepherding of some members of the congregation who would struggle with the situation. Their concerns should be understood by the leadership of the church as well as by the offender who is being welcomed to the Table. This is not the only issue where sound biblical instruction is needed to insure that justice is done while extending mercy and grace. Sometimes we can have the right theology—"the blood of Jesus Christ His Son, cleanses us from all sin" (1 John 1:7)—but we often must wrestle with the psychology of a situation. Jesus frequently calls us out of our comfort zones. This will be easier for some than for others.

One other point needs to be made, and it has to do with ministerial confidentiality. When we are providing pastoral counseling, we never promise absolute confidentiality. We do promise discretion, but we don't ever want to say, "I will never tell a soul," and then have somebody tell us where they buried the body. We reserve the full right (and moral responsibility) to call the cops if the circumstances warrant. But it is important to note that ministerial authority means that whether or not we are going to do this is a decision that rests within the church, and not with some bureaucratic functionary who has no understanding of the biblical principles of justice and mercy and how they relate. The district attorney routinely makes judgment calls regarding which crimes to prosecute or not. Likewise, church leaders make judgment calls regarding which sins rise to the level of crimes.

With regard to this topic, we have both been involved in situations where it was necessary to involve the authorities immediately. There are offenders who need to be arrested and prosecuted. But what if it was three or four five-year-olds out behind the barn being naughty? Now what? Do you call Child Protective Services over that? It is important for everyone to remember that there is more than one way to wreck a family.

All this being said, here are some key areas where remembering the principles of justice is most necessary. For various reasons, our culture has gotten to the point where we believe that neglect of these principles in matters of sex and children is actually virtuous, and that it somehow displays our moral sensitivity. Christians have unfortunately gotten swept up into some of these errors, with a little help from inflammatory indignation on the internet.

Accusation is not conviction. One of feminism's many lies is that women don't lie about rape, and the appropriate response to this is that women, as a whole, don't do anything, but that some women do lie about rape, for the same reason that some men do. Some women will lie about anything. Men, ditto. The fact that she is a woman and the subject is rape tells us nothing independent of the facts. Potiphar's wife lied about rape (Gen. 39:14). This same problem is heightened when you are dealing with children who are testifying about something—particularly when the child witness is being coached by some expert with a head full of nonsense. However, being careful about finding out the truth is not the same thing as not caring about the truth. Make no mistake, it is terrible when a child has to live within range of a sexual predator because the threshold of proof cannot be met. But it is also terrible to have a man who never did anything wrong spend ten years in prison because a child was pressured into a false accusation. The thresholds of proof in the Bible require independent confirmation of guilt. This means that, according to Scripture, in a world in which terrible things happen, the terrible thing of a guilty man going free is to be reluctantly preferred to the terrible thing of an innocent man being convicted. In addition, we find that cultures in rebellion against this standard are soon in the position of inverting other biblical standards as well—as a prelude to leveling accusations against many innocents.

The fact that someone was convicted of a sex offense does not mean that all sex offenses are in the same category of offense. We do need to have the category of statutory rape, and it needs to be policed with tough sanctions, but we also need to remember that it is a different kind of offense from the rape of a three-year-old. The latter is the kind of offense that you execute people for, and the former usually is not. It is important to distinguish, in terms of legal consequences, the creep show from the fornicator. But, returning to the point made earlier, even the creep show can be forgiven by Christ and can be served communion on death row. Sorting out this kind of thing requires true spiritual maturity, and it needs to be done by men who truly fear God. It cannot be done by linking to rants on the internet.

Once the spirit of accusation has taken root, accusations are often leveled at more than the offender. One thing we have noticed about such meltdowns is that they often occur in churches in such a way as to provide someone with the opportunity to accuse the pastors and elders who are trying to clean up the toxic waste in the aftermath. In our experience, such accusers frequently take the silence of pastors as an admission of complicity, or worse. But these snarls frequently involve many people with varying degrees of complicity, humiliation, shamed innocence, stupidity, and guilt. And it is far better for shepherds to be falsely accused than for shepherds to defend themselves by unnecessarily humiliating the sheep any further. In some situations, everything is out on the table and a pastor can talk about it freely. But in other situations, there is no way to talk about it, and no way to explain, without doing a lot more damage. To those who say that in doing this, we are "covering up," we would simply respond that we are pastors and we cover things up for a living (1 Pet. 4:8).

The church frequently must deal with the same sins and crimes that the state does. Our roles overlap and yet have distinctly different objectives. Ideally, the church and the state work together. We are happy to report that we have had some excellent experiences with the legal system in this regard (e.g., police officers, detectives, district attorneys, Child Protective Services, courts, and judges). It is a legitimate role for the state to protect all its citizens from criminals. While the state's primary objective is justice, the church's primary objective is redemption. These are not mutually exclusive concepts, but complementary. True redemption always involves justice. The church should be informed as well as aggressive in its protection of the innocent. We should be cautious, skeptical, and do our homework as all kinds of people come our way.

Nevertheless, sexual crimes are also sexual sins. Sexual crimes must be dealt with justly by the criminal courts, and sexual sins must also be dealt with by the blood of Jesus Christ. The gospel is good news for criminals, as the thief on the cross can testify. He knew that he deserved to die and that he still wanted to live. He was brought back into communion that very day.

The state's job is to provide justice. The church's job is more complicated: justice and mercy. The state's job is to protect the innocent. The church's job is to protect the innocent and to provide salvation for the guilty. We may not choose one over the other. Redemption is always about restoring bad people. Sins are always what we are being saved from, and not just the respectable sins. "Do you not know that the unrighteous will not inherit the kingdom of God? Do not be deceived. Neither fornicators, nor idolaters, nor adulterers, nor homosexuals, nor sodomites, nor thieves, nor covetous, nor drunkards, nor revilers, nor extortioners will inherit the kingdom of God. And such were some of you. But you were washed, but you were sanctified, but you were justified in the name of the Lord Jesus and by the Spirit of our God" (1 Cor. 6:9–11).

CONCLUSION

The LORD, the LORD God, merciful and gracious,
longsuffering, and abounding in goodness and truth, keeping
mercy for thousands, forgiving iniquity and transgression
and sin, by no means clearing the guilty, visiting the
iniquity of the fathers upon the children and the children's
children to the third and the fourth generation.

EXODUS 34:6-7

J ustice is an attribute of God. Without it, He could not be good. He hates evil and He punishes it. Injustice is a disruption of God's order for the world. Only justice can put the world back in order. This is true on a personal level and a cosmic level and everything in between. When justice is in place, there is goodness; when justice is perverted, misery and destruction ensue. Just judgments are God's means of restoring order in an unjust world. Moreover, justice is one of the key ways in which God demonstrates His love for us. The atonement of Christ was about satisfying God's perfect justice as He rescued unjust men. "For Christ also suffered once for sins, the just for the unjust . . ." (1 Pet. 3:18). In other words, at the heart of the gospel is the goodness *and justice* of God.

God's laws are good and just; including His instructions to us regarding the administration of justice among
ourselves and in our institutions. As children of God, we
are called to be His imitators (Eph. 5:1). His goodness is
to be our goodness, and that will necessitate justice. We
must be careful to do justice—careful for His sake, careful
for our neighbor's sake, careful for our own sake. This is
one of the chief ways we love God and love our neighbors
as ourselves. "Therefore you shall be careful to do as the
LORD your God has commanded you; you shall not turn
aside to the right hand or to the left. You shall walk in all
the ways which the LORD your God has commanded you,
that you may live and that it may be well with you, and
that you may prolong your days in the land which you
shall possess" (Deut. 5:32–33).

Speaking about Scripture, John Calvin argued that "a
perfect pattern of righteousness stands forth in the . . . one
everlasting and unchangeable rule to live by"; this holy
standard "is just as applicable to every age, even to the end
of the world."[1] His conviction is reflected in the Geneva
Confession of Faith of 1536, a confession intended for the
entire community:

> Because there is one only Lord and Master who has
> dominion over our consciences, and because his will is

1. John Calvin, *Institutes of the Christian Religion*, trans. Ford Lewis
Battles, ed. John T. McNeill, Vols. 20, 21, eds. John Baillie, John T.
McNeill, and Henry P. Van Dusen (Philadelphia: Westminster Press,
1967), (Book II, Chapter VII, section 13) 20:362.

the only principle of all justice, we confess all our life ought to be ruled in accordance with the commandments of his holy law in which is contained all perfection of justice, and that we ought to have no other rule of good and just living, nor invent other good works to supplement it than those which are there contained, as follows: Exodus 20: "I am the LORD thy God, who brought thee," and so on.[2]

THE GOSPEL AND THE JUSTICE OF GOD

The gospel sets forth the central place and importance of justice. The only just man who ever lived was unjustly crucified by a world gone mad. God's justice was satisfied in Him and then proclaimed to the world. Isaiah had prophesied of Christ,

Behold! My Servant whom I have chosen,
My Beloved in whom My soul is well pleased!
I will put My Spirit upon Him,
And He will declare justice to the Gentiles.
He will not quarrel nor cry out,
Nor will anyone hear His voice in the streets.
A bruised reed He will not break,
And smoking flax He will not quench,
Till He sends forth justice to victory;
And in His name Gentiles will trust.
(Isa. 42:1–4; 49:3; Matt. 12:18–21)

2. J.K.S. Reid, trans., "The Geneva Confession of 1536," *Reformed Confessions of the 16th Century: Edited, with Historical Introductions*, ed. Arthur C. Cochrane (Philadelphia: Westminster Press, 1966), Article 3, 120–121.

Entrusted with this gospel message, the church, above all others, must be a place where justice is done and seen. As the gospel goes forth, justice will be in its wake. Justice is ultimately about love—seeking the good of our neighbors. It is by this gospel love that the world will know that we are His disciples. Justice is indispensable. Even a pagan poet like Hesiod could see that: "When men follow justice the city blooms, the earth bears rich harvests, and children and flocks increase; but for the unjust all nature is hostile, the people waste away from famine, and a whole city may reap the evil fruit of one man's ill deeds."[3]

Righteousness and justice are the foundation of God's throne (Ps. 89:14). The new Heavens and new earth will be ruled with perfect justice; what a happy place.

> But the day of the Lord will come as a thief in the night, in which the heavens will pass away with a great noise, and the elements will melt with fervent heat; both the earth and the works that are in it will be burned up. Therefore, since all these things will be dissolved, what manner of persons ought you to be in holy conduct and godliness, looking for and hastening the coming of the day of God, because of which the heavens will be dissolved, being on fire, and the elements will melt with fervent heat? Nevertheless, we, according to His promise, look for new heavens

---

3. Hesiod, *Works and Days*, quoted in Christopher Henry Dawson, *Progress and Religion: An Historical Inquiry* (London: Sheed & Ward, 2001), 103.

and a new earth in which righteousness dwells. (2 Pet. 3:10–13)

This newness—this justice—has already begun in Christ. Let us love His justice and thereby love Him.

CONTENT ATTRIBUTIONS

This appendix identifies which of the authors is primarily responsible for the sections denoted.

INTRODUCTION: EVERYDAY JUSTICE

Booth: p. 1 to p. 4, header "Not as Easy as It Might Seem"

Wilson: p. 4 header "Not as Easy as It Might Seem" to p. 5 "...does not allow for winging it."

Booth: p. 5 "The Westminster Larger Catechism..." to p. 7 header "Injustice"

Wilson: p. 7 header "Injustice" to end of Chapter

1: CONFLICT AND JUSTICE

Wilson: p. 13 to p. 16 "...'anything done under the sun' (Eccles. 9:5-6)."

Booth: p. 16 "The man who envies desires..." to p. 17 header "The Mystery of Scandal"

Wilson: p. 17 header "The Mystery of Scandal" to end of chapter

2: STANDARDS OF JUSTICE

Booth: p. 25 to p. 28 header "The Golden Rule as a General Rule"

Wilson: p. 28 header "The Golden Rule as a General Rule" to end of chapter

3: JURISDICTION AND AUTHORITY

Booth: p. 35 to p. 37 "…care must prevail"

Wilson: p. 37 "What about the jurisdiction issues…" to end
of chapter

4: ACCUSED AND ACCUSER

Wilson: p. 41 to p.47 "…that tells you something."

Booth: p. 48 "Who is making…" to "mention their names?"

Wilson: p. 48 "And last, there is a common…" to p. 49 "This is a
common problem all over the country."

Booth: p. 49 "Spurgeon's 'John Ploughman' wrote…" to p. 50 "…
simply be round-filled."

Wilson: p. 50 "For example:…" to p. 55 header "Further Guidelines Concerning Accusations"

Booth: p. 55 header "Further Guidelines Concerning Accusations" to end of chapter

5: CHARGES AND LIES

Wilson: p. 59 to p. 63 "…that should never be lightly assumed."

Booth: p. 63 "In the midst of any controversy…" to p. 65 "…
disregard other truths."

Wilson: p. 65 "Remember, this book has to do…" to end of chapter

6: THE USE OF EVIDENCE

Booth: p. 75 to p. 77 header "We begin to unpack…"

Wilson: p. 77 header "We begin to unpack…" to end of chapter

7: WITNESSES

Booth: p. 87 to p. 89 "…nothing but the truth."

Wilson: p. 89 "No situation is so clear cut…" to p. 94 "…knows us, knows this."

Booth: p. 94 "Moreover, since 'love covers…'" to "…take the process no further."

Wilson: p. 94 "So where should we look in Scripture…" to p. 95 "…excuses are always available."

Booth: p. 95 "Another common expectation…" to "…two or three witnesses."

Wilson: p. 95 "Now think for a moment.…" to p. 102 "…assessments of their own wisdom."

Booth: p. 102 "None of this prevents a guilty person…" to end of chapter.

8: IMPUTING MOTIVES AND JUSTICE

Booth: p. 105 to p. 106 "…justice can be rendered."

Wilson: p. 106 "It is a valuable lesson to learn…" to p. 112 "…(and therefore dead) syllogisms."

Booth: p. 112 "Leaving room for the judgment…" to end of the chapter.

9: TRIAL BY INTERNET

Wilson: p. 114 to p. 116 header "No Neutrality"

Booth: p. 116 header "No Neutrality" to "…not the same thing as what you know."

Wilson: p. 116 "Here are just a few things…" to end of chapter

10: JUSTICE AND CHARACTER

Booth

11: ANONYMITY

Booth: p. 137 to p. 138 header "Nameless Others"

Wilson: p. 138 header "Nameless Others" to p. 142 header "A.K.A."

Booth: p. 142 header "A.K.A." to p. 143 "…their vocabulary are revealing."

Wilson: p. 143 "Not that identifying the voice…" to end of chapter

12: LYING, WARFARE, AND PEACE

Booth: p. 147 to p. 149 header "Deception"

Wilson: p. 149 header "Deception" to p. 153 end of page

Booth: p. 154 header "Busybodies" to p. 155 header "Pious Sentiment."

Wilson: p. 155 header "Pious Sentiment" to end of chapter

13: VICTIMS AND JUSTICE

Wilson: p. 165 to p. 175 "…it must also discipline itself."

Booth: p. 175 "Church discipline exists, in part…" to "…others take time."

Wilson: p. 175 "If someone really wants to be…" to end of page

14: DUE PROCESS

Booth: p. 177 to p. 179 header "Justice and Matthew 18"

Wilson: p. 179 header "Justice and Matthew 18 to end of chapter.

15: JUDGES AND JURIES

Wilson: p. 185 to p. 187 "…Christian before you call the cops."

Booth: p. 187 "Moreover, having sought…" to "…discipline might be called for."

Wilson: p. 187 "So we are talking about disputes…" to p. 191 "…they are charged to do this."

Booth: p. 191 "They have been duly ordained…" to p. 192 "…is of little concern to them."

Wilson: p. 192 "For some reason, what they…" to "…by any other means that occur to them."

Booth: p. 192 "Moreover, if they can get…" to "'…going to put up with that?'"

Wilson: p. 192 "If we are dealing with…" to p. 193 "…largely unquestioned and invisible."

Booth: p. 193 "A few data points are…" to p. 194 "…part of the information should not be revealed."

Wilson: p. 194 "If we know the men who…" to end of the chapter.

16: CONSCIENCE AND COURAGE

Wilson: p. 199 to p. 202 "Answers are for responsible people."

Booth: p. 202 header "Real Courage" to end of chapter.

17: THE SUPREME COURT

Booth: p. 205 to p. 210 end of page

Wilson: p. 211 top of page to end of chapter.

18: JUSTICE AND SEX ABUSE

Wilson

CONCLUSION

Booth